Draft Horses Today

*Work Horses and Mules Find Their
Way Into the 21st Century*

Draft Horses Today

*Work Horses and Mules Find Their
Way Into the 21st Century*

By
Robert A. Mischka

Heart Prairie Press
Whitewater, Wisconsin

Published by
Heart Prairie Press
P. O. Box 332
Whitewater, Wisconsin

Produced in its entirety in the United States of America.

Design, layout, and typesetting by the author on Macintosh equipment.

Publisher's Cataloging in Publication Data
    Mischka, Robert A., 1934-
      Draft horses today : work horses and mules find their way into the 21st century / Robert A. Mischka
      p. cm.
      ISBN 0-9622663-6-1

      1. Draft horses. 2. Mules. 3. Draft horses--Photographs. 4. Mules-Photographs. I. Title
SF311.M5 1992   636.15
                   QB192-512

Cover Photo: Marcus Som-Da Gus, a registered Belgian Stallion owned by Robert and Leslie Clark, makes a dramatic exit from his paddock. The Clarks raise sheep and horses on their Twin Willows Farm near Whitehall, Montana. Photo by Sally Schendel.

Dedication

To Mary, my companion and best friend for the past 40 years. It was her childhood infatuation with horses that started us down this road, and lead to a most interesting and rewarding life together.

Acknowledgements

I wish to acknowledge the debt owed by me, and by everyone connected with the draft horse scene, to Maurice Telleen. For the past 30 years Maury has provided the inspiration and glue that has held the draft horse community together.

I also want to thank the many folks who provided photos for this book; without their support and cooperation the book would have had a much more narrow focus. It was the knowledge that I had these photos, and that they should be shared, that got me going on this project.

Introduction

We bought our first draft horse, a 2-year old filly called Cantress, from Art Bast of Hartford, Wisconsin, in 1972. Our family (Mary, myself, and our five sons) had been raising and showing part-Arabs and a Quarter Horse for years. As the boys grew up and left home it was time for Dad to try something of his own — and we had a nice barn in which to do it.

Cantress' first seven foals were fillies, and the first five foals from her daughters were also fillies! We found ourselves in the draft horse business with a vengeance. We bought a stallion to breed to our fillies, and the herd grew to about 30 registered Percherons. We showed our horses at halter at most of the midwestern state fairs and quickly found out that it was quite different from showing riding horses. We had a lot to learn — so we learned.

We then began hitching our mares and showing them in harness — first in cart where we had done well with the riding horses, then as a team, and finally as a four. We started hitching our mares about the same time many shows added classes for mare hitches — a fortuitous coincidence for us. Our horses showed well in harness. Geldings out of our mares found their way into many of the successful gelding hitches throughout the United States. It was fun.

About 13 years ago we started the *Draft Horse Calendar*. We were accustomed to buying an Arabian horse calendar while raising Arabs, and were surprised to find that there wasn't a calendar featuring draft horses. So we started one. We knew nothing about publishing or printing — I am an accountant — so again we learned. The calendar has become very popular with people who own draft horses, people who remember draft horses, and people who wish they had draft horses. Through the calendar we have made literally thousands of friends, many of whom we have never met, and never will meet except through the mail.

The calendar made us realize that there was a need for draft horse materials that wasn't being satisfied. We began to try to meet this demand by telling our customers how and where they could subscribe to magazines which catered to the draft horse community. *The Draft Horse Journal* is a wonderful and indispensible magazine for draft horse enthusiasts, but we learned that some of our customers were not subscribers. Then we told our customers where they could buy draft horse books. Next we purchased the books ourselves and resold them to our customers. We then found that some of the books would go out of print, and no longer be available — so we purchased the rights to some out-of-print books and became book publishers. Finally, we began to publish some new books, as the opportunities arose.

Our mailbox contains horse pictures and stories from people from all over North America. We invite this, as we have a constant need for good pictures for our calendars. (We now have three separate calendars, the original *Draft Horse Calendar*, a *Mule Calendar*, and a light-horse *Driving Horse Calendar*.) Much of this material is very interesting, showing us how people are using their horses. Only a fraction of it can find its way into one of our calendars. Through this book we can share some of these otherwise unused pictures and stories.

This book is not a "how-to-do-it" book — there are others which do this very well. But there is a constant stream of new people getting into draft horses and they have some very basic questions, such as "What is the difference between the breeds?" and "What do you do with them?" This book will try to answer these questions.

The early chapters in this book have a considerable amount of text. Then, as I got into the chapters showing how people use their horses, it seemed to make more sense to let the pictures do the talking — so I did.

Those who are already involved with draft horses will not learn too much from this book. They probably already know more than is discussed here. But they may find enjoyment in the pictures — it may even be like a photo album of their friends and acquaintances. Seniors who pick up this book will have fun reminiscing about the "good old days", and will pick apart the mistakes they perceive being made by today's teamsters.

A few of the photos in this book have been used before in our calendars. I make no apologies for this, as I think these particular photos are outstanding and deserve to be shown again in this different setting.

Just a word about Mules. Draft mules are included in the scope of this book. I will often use the phrase "draft horses" when, in fact, I mean draft horses and draft mules. Mule fanciers are accustomed to being slighted in this way, though they don't like it very much. But it's just too cumbersome to always use the phrase "draft horses and mules". Sorry about that.

Bob Mischka

Table of Contents

The Clydesdale mare Portia, and her foal Jonesway Supreme Sadie, owned by Dan Jones of Bangor, Wisconsin. It's not a new picture, as Sadie was born in 1972, but a classic shot well worth seeing again.

Draft Horse Breeds in North America

Draft horse books usually start with a chapter containing descriptions of the various breeds. These chapters often contain definite pronouncements indicating which of the breeds is the biggest, which is the heaviest, and which is the strongest. Characterizations like these are convenient, but usually false. I'll try to avoid them.

The physical characteristics of each breed are continually changing to meet the demands of the marketplace. This is happening in all draft breeds, with the possible exception of the Suffolk. These changes are more dramatic when there are large numbers of horses to select from, such as with the Belgians; it takes much longer to make changes in breed type when there are fewer animals from which to start.

Each breed is changing to meet the demands of the marketplace.

Two broodmares and a foal from the large broodmare band owned by the Haythorn Ranch of Arthur, Nebraska. These Percheron and Belgian mares raise foals during the summer, and bring hay to the Haythorn cattle during the winter.

Two Belgian mares lead three Belgian geldings on a plow at a work-day on the Gail Deets farm in Milledgeville, Illinois. The team is owned and being driven by Calvin Simpson of Rock Falls, Illinois. Cal shows a six-horse hitch of home-grown Belgian geldings. It isn't easy to have a competitive six without including some purchased horses.

Belgians and Percherons make up about 95% of all Draft Horses in America.

The Belgian horse in North America has become taller, more stylish, and higher-stepping in the past 15 years — a direct result of the demands of today's show-hitch buyer. As a result today's Belgian is very similar to the Percheron, except for color. The occasional sorrel Percheron can easily pass for a Belgian, even among knowledgeable horsemen.

A few years ago Reginald Black, the most successful Percheron breeder in the past decade, exhibited a sorrel Percheron colt at the Michigan Great Lakes International Show. I believe that this colt could've been shown in the Belgian halter classes just as easily, and would probably have placed better than it did in the Percheron class.

These changes in type make it difficult — even foolish — to make broad, definite statements when distinguishing between the various breeds. In addition, there are as many differences between individual horses within a particular breed as there are from breed to breed. Of course there are some differences between the breeds and, like fools, we'll rush ahead and talk about them. The pictures should help.

There are five breeds of Draft Horses found in the United States — but you have to look pretty hard to find two of them. Belgians and Percherons make up about 95% of all draft horses in America. The Clydesdale is the third ranking breed, accounting for about 4% of the total. The remaining two breeds, the Suffolk and Shire, account for only about 1% of American draft horses.

BELGIANS

The Belgian draft horse, as its name implies, has its origin in Belgium, Europe. But the Belgian horse found in North America today has very little resemblance to its European ancestors, or even to the Belgian horses currently being raised in Europe. The European horse is usually a bay/roan color — and is shorter, heavier-boned, and more muscular than the horse which has evolved here.

Ann and Henry Harper raise (and import) the European-style Belgian horse at their Milkwood Farm in Orwell, Vermont. They are typical of the breeders who do not agree with the changes that have evolved (or are evolving) in their breed. These folks are to be encouraged in their resistance to changes in breed type. Changes in breed type take a long time to reverse if it is later determined that the change was a mistake, or even if some just want to go back. Without a gene pool of the "old type" it is almost impossible to go back.

Tonia, a "European-style"Belgian imported and owned by Anne and Henry Harper of Orwell, Vermont. This mare was imported as a yearling and is eighteen years old in this picture.

The typical American Belgian is a (reddish-brown) chestnut/sorrel color, preferably with a white strip down the front of the face. The fashion today is to have a white mane and tail, and four white socks. Horses colored in this way are said to have "lots of chrome".

In the 1920s there were many roan Belgians, but they are uncommon today. Bay-colored Belgians are even more rare. Blondes (light sorrel with light manes and tails) were popular about 15 years ago, but have now gone out of fashion.

A roan pulling horse owned by Mike Wiehert of Watertown, Wisconsin.

The only breed which you might confuse for a Belgian is the Suffolk. The Suffolk is always a chestnut color, including its mane and tail, but it is usually shorter and more compact than the Belgian. White markings are rare on Suffolks. When in doubt you can be pretty sure that you are looking at a Belgian, not a Suffolk, since there are so few Suffolks around.

American breeders have changed the Belgian to a tall, stylish horse with a high head-set and a snappy gait — more in keeping with today's needs for an eye-catching hitch horse. That isn't to say that there aren't a lot of the shorter, stockier horses still around. There are. The shorter, heavier "work horses" are everywhere, working on the farms, ranches and woodlots. But it is the "modern type" that now command the highest prices, and that win in the show-ring — and therefore set the "breed type" of today.

There are no reliable figures on the number of Belgian horses alive today, or even on the number of

Judy Wolf Photo

*Two Belgian geldings,
Barney and Ben, flank
the Belgian mare, Wolf's
Katie Farceur — all
owned by Richard Wolf
of Attica, New York.*

registered Belgians. However we can say that the Belgian is, by far, the most numerous of all draft breeds in North America today. With new registrations running at about 3,500 per year for the past decade, and assuming an average life span of about 14 years, you get a total of about 50,000 registered Belgians in the United States. (You can assume a different life span, but you'll come up with the same conclusion — namely that there are a lot of them.)

New registrations in Canada number about 1,000 per year, for a total of about 14,000 living registered horses, using the same formula.

Geldings are not usually registered. Grade (not pure-bred) horses are not recorded. The total of registered and non-registered Belgians in North America is probably in the neighborhood of 100,000 — give or take 10,000.

Breed Associations do not publish figures on the number of living *registered* horses, largely because horse deaths are not reported by breeders with as much punctuality as the reporting of horse births. (The Belgian Association now has about 50,000 stallions and about 81,000 mares in their active files. With 3,500 registrations per year this would give us an average life of 37 years — an unlikely possibility.)

*A team of Belgian geldings at
a pulling match keep an eye
on their competition.*

Rick Osteen Photo

Two Belgian mares and their foals from the Grupe Co. Belgians of Stockton, California. The mares exhibit the white stripes, light manes, and dark sorrel color that is fashionable today. Belgian foals often turn darker with age, and these two will probably be much darker when they are three or four. Fritz and Phyllis Grupe have come a long way since they got their first Belgian in 1976. The Grupe Co. Belgians are consistent winners at all the major shows throughout the United States, with Phyllis and David Helmuth sharing the driving. They also do a great deal of promotion for the Belgian breed, making about 50 public appearences each year (including the Rose Bowl Parade), as well as introducing school children (50,000 so far) to their Belgian horses.

5

Herbert Heiss Photo

One of the geldings from the 40-horse hitch put together by Dick Sparrow of Zearing, Iowa, half-snoozes while tied to the picket chain in the horse tent on the Milwaukee lakefront grounds. The "forty" is pictured on page 148.

Nesbitt's Misty River Ben, the main herd sire at Chapman Belgians in Tallapoosa, Georgia, is one of the outstanding Belgian sires alive today. In 1991 Ben bred 65 mares — 40 belonging to Chapman Belgians and 25 belonging to others. Bill and Myra Chapman have a strong faith in the future of the Belgian horse, and have invested in a modern breeding and foaling facility at their South Wind Farm in Tallapoosa.

Chapman Belgians Photo

A four-year old Belgian gelding owned by the late Douglas Palmer of Schomberg, Ontario, and shown at the Michigan Great Lakes International by his daughter, Beth. Doug Palmer was a "giant" in the Belgian world, both in Canada and the U.S. He died in 1991 at age 74.

Pine Grove Loretta, a Belgian mare owned by Tom Hagemann of Oak Hill Farms, Stillman Valley, Illinois. She has won Grand Champion honors at all the county fairs in northern Illinois and southern Wisconsin, and has placed well at some National shows. She is a good cart horse, and is now raising foals who are carrying on her winning tradition.

PERCHERONS

The Percheron Horse originated in the La Perche district of France. Like the Belgian, it has evolved here into quite a different horse than is now being raised in France. The American Percheron is taller, with a longer neck and a "hitchier" appearance than found today in France.

A pair of young Percheron stallions in a pasture in the La Perche district of France.

This difference is not surprising, given the different needs for which the horses are being bred in America versus France. The main market for French Percherons is the horse-meat market. I visited the main government breeding farm for Percheron Stallions at Le Pin, France in 1986 and asked the employees "What are these (Percheron) horses used for these days?" I was told that they were raised for meat. This was a little disheartening, so I asked if there might be some other use, in addition to the meat trade. The answer was no. With this emphasis it is not surprising that the French Percheron is shorter and heavier than that currently desired in America.

There have been very few Percherons imported into North America from France in the past decade. Exceptions that come to mind were a stallion to Lucasia Ranch in Alberta and several horses to Clarence Dudley in California. Their main value has been as an outcross to the domestic bloodlines. The predominant draft horse in France is not the Percheron, but the Ardennes, and there are nine distinct draft breeds in France.

A meat market in Paris — one of many there which feature horsemeat.

Percherons come in two colors, grey and black. Grey horses typically start out as jet black when they are born, and end up completely white in their old age. In between they can be all shades of grey, from almost black with a few white hairs, an all-over steel grey, black with white mane and tail, dapple grey, or "flea-bitten" grey. Bay Percherons are rare, and sorrels even rarer. (Bay and sorrel Percherons are also confusing. Now that there is little conformation difference between the Belgian and Percheron breeds it might be time to discourage the registration of Percherons which are not black or grey.)

Today's "modern" Percheron tends to be an upstanding, hitchy animal with lots of class. Those who prefer the shorter, heavier, more compact animal refer to the newer type in a disparaging way as a "coach

Virginia Thorne Photo

Molly and Dolly, a team of bay Percheron mares owned by John Colby of Eagle, Wisconsin. John did everything with this pair. It would be hard to find a sweeter team to work with. On page 52 they are plowing a garden.

A team of black Percheron geldings owned by Fred Mason of Whitewater, Wisconsin. Fred is a dairy-farmer who keeps a team of horses for local parades and shows.

The grey Percheron stallion, Blizzard, being shown at the Toronto Royal Winter Fair by the late Joseph Michalyshen of Brandon, Manitoba. Blizzard was named grand Champion at many shows, including Toronto. He was bred by Bob and Marilyn Robinson of Richland, Michigan, by South Valley Did-It out of Princess. This mating has produced many outstanding horses for the Robinsons, including five Grand Champions at the Toronto Royal Winter Fair.

The Percheron was the preferred breed until the 1930's, outnumbering all other breeds combined by four to one.

horse" — not a draft horse. This situation (no clear agreement on type) is similar to that which is found in the Belgian breed. Both types can be found in both breeds.

It boils down to the difference between a work horse and a show horse. There is general agreement that the shorter, heavier, more compact horse will do more work, and require less feed, than will the other. This creates a demand for that type among those who use their horses for work. It is also generally true that the taller, leggier, higher stepping, showier horse will look flashier in the show-ring or in a parade. This creates a demand for that type among those who use their horses for recreation or advertising. Since the latter type is also the type that is winning in the show-ring it is easy to assume that it is the official "breed type". But the results would be different if the judging was being done at field workdays, or on the farm, or in the woodlots. Ideal type is an elusive concept — it depends on the intended use.

The Percheron is the second most popular draft horse in America. This wasn't always the case. The Percheron was, by far, the preferred breed until the mid 1930s. During much of the time when draft horses were the major source of power — from the 1880's to the 1930's — Percherons outnumbered all other breeds combined by three to one! The decline in draft horses during the 40s and 50s hit the Percherons hardest since the Amish kept their horses, and they preferred the Belgian. Thus, when the draft horse "came back" in the 70s the Belgian was in a better position to increase — and it did so. A friend referred to this relatively recent upsurge in Belgian numbers, as opposed to Percherons, by saying "The Belgian horse was invented after all the work had been done (by Percherons)."

Again, there are no reliable figures on the number of living registered Percherons, since the Association records include many animals that have died. One approach to determine the number would be to start with the number of horses registered between 1970 through 1990 — a total of 16,000 mares and stallions. Assuming that 25% of these animals are now dead you would have 12,000 living *registered* horses. Adding something for the (unregistered) geldings and grade Percherons you come up with about 25,000 Percherons, give or take 5,000.

Ardfair's Royal Jason, winner of the Percheron gelding class at a recent Michigan Great Lakes International Show, exhibited and owned by Bill Hassard of Stouffville, Ontario. Jason exhibits the long leg and trim appearance which is winning in the showring today. His mother and full sister have also been Grand Champions at the Great Lakes Show. Pedigrees are just as important with geldings as they are with breeding animals.

The Percheron stallion, Maverick, owned by Art & Hazel Bast of Hartford, Wisconsin, and shown here at the Michigan Great Lakes International Show by their son, Jon. Maverick was not only a good breeding stallion, he also showed to Grand Champion honors at all the major shows and was a good hitch horse. It is a little unusual when a stallion will halter well, breed well, and hitch. Art used Maverick to break young colts, and he was a mainstay in their hayride business.

Ed Carlson (left) and Dave Adams of Britt, Iowa, showing four of Dave's hitch geldings at the Belvidere, Illinois show. Dave's horses dominated the hitch classes for many years, winning all the major shows in both the United States and Canada. Dave is now managing and driving the Waverly Midwest Horse Sale Percheron hitch.

A Percheron mare and her foal at the Mischka Farm. This foal already exhibits the long leg that breeders seek today to get the taller show-horse. The mare is 18 hands tall. The foal has a lot of growing to do, but it already has most of its cannon bone between the knee and hoof.

12

CLYDESDALES

The Clydesdale horse originated in the valley of the Clyde River near Glasgow, Scotland. The Clydesdale horse being bred in Scotland today is the type still sought by American breeders. Each year many breeders make visits to Scotland to attend the shows and purchase Clydesdales for export to America.

The Clydesdale is, of course, the "Budweiser horse". The use of the Clydesdale as a marketing technique to sell Budweiser beer is one of the classic advertising successes — and is taught and analyzed in every basic college course on advertising. Everyone knows about the "Budweiser horses". Those of us who have met the public at our stalls at state fairs or other horse shows have become accustomed to having our Percherons, Belgians, etc. described as "Budweiser horses". I do it myself. When someone asks what kind of horse we raise I reply "Percherons". If that brings nothing but a blank stare, I usually follow up with "They're work horses, like the Budweiser horses, but a different color." That usually elicits an appropriate response.

Clydes can be black, roan, or bay, with the "Budweiser Bay" the most common. The feather, or long hairs above the hooves, is usually white. This feather is one of the distinguishing characteristics of Clydesdales — a trait they share with the Shires. A wide white strip (blaze) down the front of the face is desirable.

Because of their feather the Clydes are very flashy when trotting or parading — the feather accentuates their action by calling attention to their hooves when they trot. But there is a downside to this feather as well. The long hairs tend to collect dirt and mud, and are difficult to keep clean. Because of this the Clyde is not used as a work horse as frequently as some of the other breeds.

Again, there are no reliable figures on the number of Clydes. But with registrations currently running at about 400 per year, we can guess that there might be in the neighborhood of 5,000 registered Clydes in the United States. This breed is growing quite rapidly, as there were only 200 registrations per year just 10 years ago. Growth is a relative thing — when you start from near zero it is easier to double each year. In the Belgian association an increase of 200 registrations per year wouldn't be noticed.

The general public calls all draft horses "Budweiser horses"

A young pair of Clyde geldings owned by David Stalheim of Amery, Wisconsin. Dave is a dairy-farmer who raises Clydesdales as a hobby, as his father did before him. Note the unusual hand-made hame-tops on Dave's harness

Beth Fornaro Photo

A pair of Clydesdale hitch geldings enjoy a little rest and recreation between assignments. Ten years ago it seemed that Budweiser had all the good, big, Clyde hitch geldings. Now there are many good Clyde hitches on the road and at the shows — the most improvement of all the draft breeds in hitch horses during the last decade.

David Carson with his team of Clyde geldings at the Boone County Fair in Belvidere, Illinois. David is from Listowel, Ontario, where he farms and operates a livestock and real estate auction business. With him on the seat is Marion Young.

Dr. Michael Moleski of Bronson, Michigan, accepts the trophy for Joey as the Champion Clydesdale gelding at the 1989 Michigan Great Lakes International Show. Presenting the trophy is Amy Schmitz, the 1989 Michigan Draft Horse Breeder's Queen. Joey was twice the Champion Clyde gelding at Detroit, once at the National Clyde Show, and the winner of his class at the Toronto Royal Winter Fair. He is now eleven years old, and is winning in cart classes and serving as a wheel horse on the Moleski's four- and six-horse hitches.

SHIRES

The Shire horse has its origins in England. It was developed as a war horse to carry heavily armored knights into battle. In the 1800s the Shire was no longer needed in war and it became important in commerce and agriculture. It is still used as a ceremonial horse in affairs of the Crown and for publicity purposes by some of the major breweries in England, much as the Clyde is used by Budweiser in America.

There have been many importations of Shires into the United States in the past 10 years, with most of them coming to the Fox Valley Draft Horse Farm in Marengo, Illinois. This farm, under the ownership of Thomas Smrt, now has the largest concentration of Shire Horses in the World, with about 500 English Shires.

The phrase "English Shire" is used to denote horses registered in England. There is an attempt by some to downplay or discredit horses registered by the American Shire Registry, and to consider only horses registered by the English Shire Registry as true registered Shire horses. This is unfortunate. Shires have been imported into the United States since the late 1800s, and the American Shire Registry has been in existence for over 100 years.

The largest concentration of Shire Horses in the World (500 horses) is in Marengo, Illinois.

Shires come in many colors, including black, brown, bay, grey, and chestnut. Most Shires in the United States are grey, black, or bay. A bald face and white stockings are preferred markings on black Shires. Excessive white markings and roaning are undesireable.

Bosley Minn's Gillian, Grand Champion Shire mare at the Michigan Great Lakes International (twice), the Ohio State Fair, the Canadian National Exposition, and many other shows. She was imported from England as a two year old in 1988, along with her half-brother, Swallow Hill Sir Andrew, by John and Judith McNish of Maple Run Shires, Newbury, Ohio. Gillian is pictured being shown by Judith McNish at the 1991 Great Lakes International.

Jack Schatzberg Photo

A young Shire stallion in his pasture at the Fox Valley Farm, Marengo, Illinois. Fox Valley Farm is also the home of Shireland, a theme park designed to promote the English Shire horse.

The Shire is a "feathered" breed (like the Clydesdale), with fine, long hairs on the lower leg making a very showy appearance at the trot.

Shires are similar to, and difficult to tell apart from, Clydesdales. Generally the Shire is a heavier-boned, more massive animal — but this is a generalization only, with many exceptions. There has been plenty of crossbreeding between Clydes and Shires in the past — and still today — for the gelding market. (Since geldings are not registered animals, their parentage is, unfortunately, often not considered important). Shires and Clydesdales are frequently shown together (against each other) in halter classes. Some Clyde hitch horses are, in fact, part Shire.

There are about 2,500 Shire horses in the United States, with about 500 of them at the Fox Valley Draft Horse Farm.

Doug Hutchins Photo

Donna Thomas plowing with four Shire horses owned by her and her parents, Mel and Dorothy Anderson of Ellensburg, Washington. These are good examples of the American Shire horse, as opposed to the English Shires pictured on the preceeding page. The Shire was a popular work horse during the early years of this century, and the descendants of those horses are still found working on many farms and ranches in the western United States today.

SUFFOLKS

The Suffolk draft horse comes from England, where it is called the Suffolk Punch. It has suffered more than any other breed in the switch from horsepower to tractor power, as it was bred almost exclusively as a farm draft animal. There are only about 100 registered Suffolks left in England, and the breed has been placed in the *Critical* category by England's Rare Breeds Survival Trust.

Several years ago I visited a farmer in England who did all his work with horses, using Percherons and Ardennes. I asked him why he had no Suffolks, the English farm horse. He expressed his opinion that the breed had declined so much in numbers that it no longer had the genetic diversity to allow it to continue, and he thought the breed was on its way to extinction. Suffolk breeders in England have debated the merits of importing a stallion or two from America to increase their genetic pool, and perhaps improve their conception rate, but their pride has, so far, prevented such a "drastic" move.

In England you have several large Breweries breeding Shires and using them for advertising, and you have a steady demand for Clydes from America — but there is no similar underpinning to the Suffolk breed. Suffolk breeders described their horse as "The Only Draft Horse Bred for the Furrow" — and their horse was replaced by the tractor.

Little Creek Sand Lilly, an eight-yr old Suffolk mare, and her eight-week old filly, Cumberland's Foxy, in a field of daffodils on the Cumberland Suffolk Farm near Crossville, Tennessee. Note the long tail on the mare. Suffolk breeders, and many Clyde and Shire breeders, do not dock the tails on their horses.

There are only about 100 registered Suffolks left in England.

Suffolks are chestnut in color. How simple and tidy. The chestnut color can range from light golden to dark liver — but it is still chestnut. Few white markings are found, and those that are found are usually a star, snip, or a little white about the pasterns.

Most American Suffolk breeders have resisted the current "bigger is better" fashion found in the other breeds. As a result the typical Suffolk is only slightly taller than 16 hands. This is quite small in comparison to the other draft breeds, and is definitely one of the Suffolk's distinguishing characteristics. They typically have a pleasant, well-balanced, almost "sweet" look about them. They have the reputation as having a good disposition and being easy to work with.

Suffolk owners are quick to point out that their (smaller) horses can do (almost) the same amount of work as the other breeds, at considerably less feed cost. This is probably true. It is generally agreed that the smaller, more compact draft horse in any breed can outwork a taller, bigger horse, while requiring much less feed.

There are about 500 Suffolks in the United States. This is far more than in their native land, England, but still not very many. They would be classified as an "endangered species" if the organizations who concern themselves with such things included domesticated animals in their surveys. Most Suffolk breeders feel a responsibility to promote and strengthen the breed, and are working hard to do so.

A team of Suffolk geldings. Suffolks have quite a different look about them, particularly in their heads, from other draft breeds. Note the nylon harness which is manufactured by Deb Evans at her harness shop in Crossville, Tennessee. Nylon harness weighs less and is easier to care for than the traditional leather harness.

A team of Suffolk geldings pull a trolley loaded with visitors at the Kentucky Horse Park in Lexington, Kentucky. The Horse Park is a wonderful place to visit, with a horse museum that is world class. I don't know where else you will see all the major draft breeds together in a single pasture.

Two mules cultivating between the rows at the Matt Tures Sons Nursery near Huntley, Illinois. This particular pair has been doing this work from mid-May to mid-August each year — for the past 17 years!

DRAFT MULES

Draft Mules are large harness mules — as opposed to saddle mules — usually obtained by crossing a draft mare to a donkey stallion, or jack. The largest draft mules are the result of crossing a draft mare to a Mammoth Jack, a particular breed of donkey developed specifically for this purpose. Draft Mules can be all shapes, colors, and sizes — since their parents also can be all shapes, colors, and sizes.

Since we have started our Mule Calendar two years ago I have come to appreciate the good qualities of mules. They are remarkable animals with an undeserved bad reputation. Those who take the time to become friends with mules really like them.

Mules aren't show-biz animals. A class of six-mule hitches trotting (looks more like prancing) around a coliseum won't quicken your heartbeat, or make your blood run faster, as a similar class of Belgians or Percherons might. But mules will do what needs to be done, for less money (feed and vet bills), and far less fuss, than will horses. There are good reasons why the U.S. Park service uses mules to take tourists up and down the Grand Canyon wall — they can be trusted to do this dangerous job in a safe and sane manner.

A mule can't be bullied into doing something he doesn't want to do, or into something he doesn't understand. Horses can. As a result many horse people have unpleasant experiences when they try their hand at mule training. It seems that people either love or actively dislike mules — there is no middle ground. The mule, like a dog, can instantly tell when a person doesn't like it — and it reacts accordingly. It is important that mules be trained by someone who understands and likes them. They are suspicious by nature, and must learn to trust people. This cannot be learned from trainers with harsh methods.

Mules have strange and silly-sounding voices — at least it seems that way when you first hear them. But I suspect that mule fanciers don't hear it that way. It also occurs to me that the horse has a rather strange voice too, and that it probably seemed odd when I first heard it. The movies and TV condition us to the sound of horse's voices from an early age — but not to the braying of mules. I suppose that because a mule looks similar to a horse we expect it to sound like one. It doesn't.

20

SUMMARY

The choice of a particular draft breed is a personal one. There is no right or wrong choice. The most important thing is to pick a breed, and an individual within the breed, that pleases you. If you're going out to the barn twice a day you want to be greeted by animals which you enjoy.

The breeds with large numbers (Belgians and Percherons) have more animals to pick from, making it easier to find good ones at lower prices. It's just a matter of supply and demand. Of course the same thing is true, in reverse, if later you are a seller looking for a buyer.

Before we leave the subject of breeds it should also be mentioned that there are many other draft breeds in the world in addition to those found in North America. The ones we have just described simply happen to be those that were imported to the United States and Canada during the period 1880 to 1920 and have found a home here. It wouldn't make much sense to try to establish another breed in America — and you'd have to have pretty deep pockets to try — but we shouldn't ignore the fact that there are many other draft breeds in other countries. We have recently published a book called *Heavy Horses of the World* which describes other draft breeds for those wishing to pursue this topic further.

A team of 17-hand molly mules owned by Vernon Cornett of Jeffrey, West Virginia, waiting to enter the showring at the Michigan Great Lakes International Show. These are unusually big mules.

Of course you don't have to pick just one breed. Here George Andrew of Eagle Bridge, New York, is cutting grain with his restored Deering Sweep Rake Reaper using a five-yr old Belgian mare (chestnut) and a six-yr old gelding that is 3/4 Belgian and 1/4 Percheron.

A Percheron team in the ring at the Waverly Midwest Horse Sale, Waverly, Iowa. The red numbers behind the team, on the far wall, indicate that there are two horses being sold, and that the current bid is $1,400 each.

Draft Horse Auctions

THE NUMBERS ARE STAGGERING

Draft horse and mule folks have a love affair with horse auctions. Each year more than 10,000 animals are sold at draft horse auctions, with a combined sales value approaching $20,000,000. This is a big business!

The two largest sales are the Waverly Midwest Sale in Waverly, Iowa and the Topeka Livestock Sale in Topeka, Indiana. These two sales are both held twice a year, in the spring and fall. They regularly sell 800 to 1,000 animals, for a total value of well over $1 million dollars, at each of these four sales.

Another major sale is the Eastern States Draft Horse Sale held at the Ohio State Fairgrounds in Columbus, Ohio — where 700 to 800 horses are sold each February. The Reese Brothers Mule Sale held in Dixon, Tennessee, sells about 1,000 mules twice each year. The totals for just

> More than 10,000 animals are sold at draft horse auctions each year.

This team of Percheron geldings sold under the brigtly colored tent at the Lester Detweiler auction near Brodhead, Wisconsin, for $2,350 each.

A young team of Belgian colts selling at an Arnold Hexom sale in Waterloo, Iowa.

Smokey Lynn Bare will, for a fee, decorate your horse before it goes into the sale ring — if you need those services. Smokey breeds Thorodale and Clydesdale horses at her farm in Westerville, Ohio.

these four auctions (seven sales) amount to over 6,000 animals and about $10,000,000 each year. *The Draft Horse Journal* carries ads for over 30 other auctions in each quarterly issue.

Many individuals both buy and sell horses at the same auction. But it would be a mistake to think that this fact, in any way, reduces the "big business" aspect of the auctions. The horses you purchased have to be paid for, in cash, long before you receive the money for those you have sold. If the sales at the two-day Columbus Sale total $1.2 million then the people hanging around the sale ring, buying horses, must pay out that amount of cash at the end of the two day period. This is a little surprising, as the people at draft horse sales don't look as though they could come up with that kind of money. Oh, there are some buyers from Japan or from a South American country at ringside, or a businessman with deep pockets who needs some horses for his show hitch, at the larger sales. But most of the buyers are farmers, wearing overalls and barn-boots — not a group of Middle East oil magnates and rich movie stars attending a Kentucky thoroughbred auction. But they do it, year after year, over and over again.

AUCTION PROCEDURES

The sales fall into two basic types. Most sales allow the seller to "no-sale" his animal if he doesn't think that the final bid is high enough. In those cases the seller usually pays a sales commission to the auction house as he would if the horse were actually sold. Sometimes the "no-sale" commission is less than it would be if the horse was sold at that same price.

Other sales, like the Columbus Sale, are absolute auctions where the animal is transferred to the last bidder, regardless of the amount. A friend or neighbor can be set-up beforehand to do some bidding if the animal seems to be selling too cheap. But if the friend or neighbor ends up as the buyer, and the horse is a registered animal, this deception is easy to detect by checking the registration records to find animals that are later transferred back to the original owner. Consignors caught doing this are not invited back.

Top: *A view of the Eastern States Draft Horse Sale at Columbus, Ohio, from the door where the horses enter and leave. A Belgian gelding is being sold in the ring, while other Percheron and Belgian geldings wait their turn.*

Bottom: *Another view of the Eastern State Sale, this time looking east toward the door where the horses enter and leave. The auctioneer's booth is on the left side of the picture. The building is crowded, loud, hot, and humid, but the excitement and drama keep the spectators glued to their seats, hour after hour.*

Most of the larger auctions have some provision for inspecting the sale animals, and for calling out any unsoundness or defect found in this inspection when the horse is sold. Broke horses are typically hitched the day before they are sold, and the way they behaved during hitching is also called out by the auctioneer or pedigree man. Mares which are sold as pregnant must be accompanied by a Health Certificate testifying to that fact, or they are examined by a veterinarian at the sale before being sold. Horses usually must have certain shots before coming to the sale, and need Health Certificates to prove that the shots have been administered. Registered horses need to have their registration papers in order before they can be sold as such. All these procedures are set forth in the sales instructions and the catalogs (issued at the bigger sales).

These sale catalogs are a project in themselves. The 1991 Columbus Sale Catalog contains 192 pages of pedigrees, descriptions, and information relating to over 700 horses and their owners. All horses sold at Columbus are listed in the catalog, and are entered in the sale some three months before the sale date. Other sales, such as Waverly and Topeka, sell both cataloged and uncataloged horses. Cataloged horses are sold first, in the order they appear in the catalog, followed by those not listed. It takes a good deal of detective work to learn anything about the uncataloged horses, as it is hard to know where they are in the sale barn before they hit the sale ring.

The Waverly Midwest Horse Sale site in Waverly, Iowa, with the machinery lot at the upper left, the camper lot at the upper right, and the horse barn, pens, and sales barn in the center right. A crowd of people are bidding on harness in front of the red doors in the center of the picture.

At Waverly there is a "killer pen" for horses destined for the slaughterhouse. These horses are sold at the end of the sale, and do not have to be accompanied by their owner into the sale ring. More than one horse has been rescued from that fate by a knowledgeable horseman and converted into a useful animal.

Single draft horses are usually sold wearing a halter, and led by a handler. A "whip man" often trails the horse to encourage him to trot smartly in

Teams to be sold as broke are hitched in the yard outside the Waverly Sale barn each morning of the sale, and graded on their manners by sale personnel. The result of this grading is announced by the auctioneer when they are sold.

the ring. Draft teams are often sold in pairs, wearing harness. With a pair of horses the last bidder usually has the option of taking his choice of the two horses, or both. The amount the auctioneer is asking for, and the amount he gets as his final bid, is always "per horse". At a certain point in the bidding a pair of horses are sometimes "tied together", and the buyer must take them both. It frequently happens when a buyer takes his choice of a pair that the second horse, presumably the less desirable one, sells for more money than did the first — an example of what makes auctions fascinating to the student of human nature. At mule auctions the animals are usually sold more like cattle or other livestock — herded in the sales arena without any halters or harness.

It is important to understand the terminology at a horse auction. It can be expensive if you're bidding and don't understand what the auctioneer means when he announces something from the box. And the words he uses to describe the horse he is selling can change from year to year. For example, for years the auctioneers at the Columbus Sale would describe horses with sidebones as "a little hard on the corners". Currently

This young man is demonstrating how gentle and easy to handle his team is by riding them Roman-style in the Waverly Sale ring.

a horse with sidebones is described as being "serviceably sound". *(Sidebones is a hardening of the arteries and cartilage at the rear of the hoof, above the coronary band, particularly on the front feet. Some believe that this condition will lead to contracted heels, and eventual lameness. It was a bigger problem years ago when horses spent their lives pulling loads over hard pavements.)* This change in terminology reflects a change in the way the sidebone defect is considered today, considering the use to which today's draft horse is generally put. It illustrates that you must be aware of what the auctioneer says, and that he means by what he says. The phrases used by the auctioneer are not defined in the catalog. If you don't understand what the auctioneer means by a particular word it would be wise to ask someone who does.

Arnold Hexom

The Waverly Sale is like a great big family reunion.

Arnold Hexon (right) with the grey stetson he always wore, doing what he loved — calling a draft horse auction. This was at the Waterloo Dairy Cattle grounds in Waterloo, Iowa, where Arnold held his own auction for a few years after his split with Bill Dean at Waverly.

HORSE SALE PERSONALITIES

The father of draft horse auctions was Arnold Hexom. Arnold started the Waverly sale in 1948, a time when the draft horse business was just about non-existent. He was a horseman — a man who truly loved horses — who also happened to be an auctioneer. There was nothing he'd rather do than call a draft horse sale. And he called hundreds of them, including his own, until his death in 1990 at the age of 77.

I bought my second draft horse at the Waverly Sale, with Arnold doing the auctioneering. At that time the sale was held in a tent, with the horses dodging the center tent poles. I was bidding on a black gelding to hitch with our mare. Arnold felt that the horse, named Jed (pictured on page 131), was going too cheap so he kept throwing in a bid of his own. He finally quit at $725, and for $750 the horse was mine. Arnold immediately told me (and everyone else in the tent) that if at the end of the day I didn't like the horse he would buy him from me and give me a $50 profit. This made me feel good, as if I really had gotten a bargain, and probably eased his conscience for bidding against me. (*Perhaps I should've taken him up on his offer, as Jeb turned out to have ringbone, and wasn't sound very long — but this is something he would have been unable to tell from the auction box.*)

Arnold was well liked — even loved — by most people with whom he came in contact. He would call the Waverly Sale for 12 hours straight with nothing but an occasional swig of orange juice from the covered mason jar alongside him on the table. Then, after a short break for food and a stop at the restroom he would be back for another six hours on the box. The next morning he would be back and do it all over again!

Arnold loved to tell stories, and he was a great joker. He owned a six horse hitch of grey Percherons which he took to many of the midwestern fairs. Arnold loved to sit in the fairground horse barns in the evening, near his beloved horses, and trade stories and jokes with anyone who would listen — all night long. It was the culmination of one of his dreams when his hitch of six greys driven by Jim Meyer, appeared in the Rose

Bowl Parade — and another when they were the first six from the United States to win at the Toronto Royal Winter Fair.

Arnold Hexom was a giant in the draft horse community. He had a profound influence on the entire draft horse industry. I, and hundreds of others, miss him. It seemed like a tragedy when Arnold sold out his share in the Waverly Sale to his partner, Bill Dean, in 1972, and a few years later left the Waverly scene altogether. But as it turned out, Bill and Elsie Dean rose to the challenge and have made the Waverly Sale both bigger and better than ever. The Waverly Sale is a model of organization and planning. There are many employees both inside and out, and they are efficient and knowledgeable in what they do. The grounds are neat and well planned, and there is a minimum of confusion despite the large crowds which attend.

Bill Dean taking his turn at the auction mike during the machinery portion of his Waverly Midwest Sale.

The Waverly Sale is somewhat unique in that it is now, and always has been, owned and run by the fellow doing the auctioneering. At most other sales the sale management hires the auctioneer. This gives an added personal touch to the Waverly Sale.

Each year dozens of folks who haven't had horses for years (and who have no plans to own them in the future) make their semi-annual pilgrimage to the Waverly Sale. They arrive with their campers, hook up to one of the 400 camper hookups Bill and Elsie have provided, and spend the whole week enjoying the activities. They catch up on the latest gossip and tell horse stories (over and over again) to whoever will listen. It's like a great big family reunion. Vacations and work are planned around the Waverly Sale, as in "The corn tested 23% moisture, so I figured that after Waverly it would be just about right."

The first annual auction of Shires at the Fox Valley Farm held in October, 1991, had a theatrical atmosphere, with ringside tables and horses in spotlights, all under the big red circus tent at Shireland near Marengo, Illinois.

The Columbus Sale is put on each year by the Ohio Belgian and the Ohio Percheron Associations. In other words, it is put on by a bunch of horse breeders — mostly farmers — on a volunteer basis. This gives it a somewhat different "flavor" than some of the other sales. (Each sale seems to have its own personality.) It is more low key, with less hype and show-biz, than some of the other big sales. As Bill Westbrook puts it, "The

Kim Sigmon with a pair of Windmill Acres mares in the sale arena at the Dixie Draft Horse & Mule Sale held at the Dixie Classic Fairgrounds in Winston-Salem, North Carolina.

A pair of bay geldings being sold at the Waverly Sale for $3,000 each by Freeman Detweiler, Jr. to Jim & Sue Kane. These geldings are now doing daily duty in the Kane's carriage ride business (see page 112). The Kanes did their homework on these horses before the sale, and came with the intention of buying them.

Columbus Sale is put on by a bunch of amateurs." But it doesn't seem amateur, as the people who run it have learned what works and what doesn't work in the 30 years this sale has been held.

Bill Reed (Past-President of the Percheron Association of America) heads up the Sale Committee, Dr. A. F. Allen (current President of the Belgian Draft Horse Corporation of America) is in charge of assigning stalls, Sally Reed (Bill Reed's daughter-in-law) handles the Secretary duties, and Bill Westbrook takes care of the horse and hitching inspections. Each of these individuals (except for Sally) has been doing their job for many, many years — and they know what they are doing. In the case of Sally, she replaced Orlefa Loyer a few years ago, but Orlefa is still on hand in the office during the sale to help out as needed. No, these people aren't amateurs. They are professionals, who do this work on a part-time, volunteer basis. The Columbus Sale is the most prestigious of all the draft horse sales.

HORSE-DRAWN MACHINERY AUCTIONS

A few scenes from the machinery lot at the Waverly Midwest Horse Sale — the largest horse-drawn machinery auction in America.

Just fifteen years ago draft horse owners had a hard time finding the machinery and tools they needed to do the things they wanted to do with their horses. This is no longer true. Most of the larger draft horse sales begin with a sale of horse-related machinery.

At the Waverly Sale you will find virtually anything you can think of that relates to horses — and a lot of it. It takes two full days, with two rings going, to complete the machinery auction. Over 1,800 bidder numbers are issued for the machinery sale, with over 9,000 items changing hands during the two days.

Fifteen years ago Waverly would have 2 or 3 horse-drawn manure spreaders. At the last sale there were 34 spreaders, ranging in condition from poor to brand-new. Other examples at a recent Waverly sale were four horse-drawn hearses, 20 mowers, 2 threshing machines, 50 heavy wheel running gears, 2 hay loaders, over 50 sleighs and cutters — and the list goes on and on.

It boggles the mind to think of the time and effort involved in hauling all this "stuff" to Waverly twice each year, from literally all parts of the country and many parts of Canada — and then hauling it all away again to be used (or stored) by the new owners.

SUMMARY

I think it is better for newcomers to draft horses to buy their first horse from an established breeder at his farm, rather than at an auction. Buying a horse is a lot like buying a used car — the seller knows a lot more about it than does the buyer, and therefore has an advantage. At the breeder's farm some of this advantage is eliminated. At the farm it's easier to ask the seller questions than it is at the auction barn. It's a more relaxed situation at the farm, and you usually can see the parents and siblings of the horse you are considering. You can take your time in a farm situation — make several visits — and return with a friend for a second opinion. The reputable breeder has his reputation to consider, and will not knowingly sell a horse with a serious defect without making sure the buyer is aware of the defect. It is no secret that some horses sold through auctions are animals that the owner was unable to sell privately due to some unsoundness or defect.

One way to have the best of both worlds — the farm situation and the auction price-setting mechanism — is to send for the sale catalog, study it at home to locate those horses that seem to be what you want, and then visit those horses at the owner's farm before they are taken to the auction. You can then become a more informed, knowledgeable bidder at the auction.

It's hard to tell whether these gentlemen are examining the merchandise or visiting. A lot of both takes place at draft horse auctions.

Horse sales have become more than a place to buy or sell horses. They have become a gathering place for those involved in the draft horse scene. Horsemen from literally all over the country attend them on a regular basis, regardless of whether they have something to sell or buy. People just automatically assume that you will be at the Columbus Sale each February — or if you are absent that you must have a good excuse.

The draft horse auction is an exciting event — especially if you like horses and/or people. There is drama, color, comedy, danger, excitement, and money involved in every auction. It gets in your blood, and becomes a habit. If you haven't attended one you should try it. If you have, then you know what I'm talking about.

*Wayne Randall binding oats with three
Percherons on the Merle Fischer farm near
Jefferson, Wisconsin — a job that isn't possible
without their "antique" grain binder. It is
surprising that there are so many grain
binders still in existence, since none have been
manufactured for over 50 years.*

Joe Mischka Photo

Draft Horse Vehicles and Equipment

A prerequisite to the use of draft horses is the availability of horse-drawn vehicles and equipment. Here in North America we are blessed with an abundance of such equipment, largely due to the talents of, and demands from, the Amish and Mennonite communities.

Draft horse owners in other countries are not similarly blessed. The use of draft horses for farming in England, for example, is severly limited by a lack of horse-drawn farm machinery. I really didn't understand this until recently when I learned that there are no Amish or Mennonite peoples in Europe, and that there haven't been any there for over 120 years. When the conversion from horses to tractors took place in Europe in the 1920-40 period the conversion was complete, without a nucleus of hard-core horse farmers to slow the trend or keep the old ways alive.

> We are blessed with an abundance of horse-drawn machinery due, in large part, to the resourcefulness of the Amish and Mennonite communities.

Paul Cleland of Reading, Michigan is spreading his manure with a brand-new spreader made by the E-Z Spreader Mfg. Co. of Sugarcreek, Ohio. This spreader is similar to the New Idea 10A spreader.

FARM MACHINERY

About ten years ago the New Idea Company announced that they were going to stop manufacturing their Model 10A horse-drawn manure spreader. This really upset me, and I wrote several letters to the company trying to convince them that this was a short-sighted decision, and how their sales of this machine were bound to increase in the future. They weren't convinced by my arguments, and wouldn't change their mind.

Jim Cleland Photo

The White Horse Machine Co. of Gap, Pennsylvania, makes a very fine horse-drawn plow. It features a ground-driven hydraulic cylinder which lifts the plow at the end of the row as well as a trip-reset mechanism which is activated whenever a rock or other solid object is hit.

Kim Kraemer raking hay with a team of Percherons owned by the author. Kim is sitting on a conventional forecart, using it to pull a side-delivery rake with a tractor drawbar.

I then saw it as a business opportunity, and decided that I should buy up all the spare parts for this spreader and go into the 10A rebuilding business. I didn't follow through on this idea, lacking both the expertise and time. But the E-Z Spreader Mfg Co. in Sugarcreek, Ohio had both, and they now produce a new Model 10A spreader and provide spare parts for existing ones. Other companies have sprung up to recondition existing spreaders, and at least one other company (Millcreek) produces a new ground-driven, four-wheel spreader.

Last year the apron chain on my 10A spreader rusted out, and needed to be replaced. I drove down to my local New Idea dealer and asked him to order me an apron chain, as I knew it was too much to expect him to have one in stock. He was incredulous that someone would still be using one of those spreaders. He refused to believe me when I said that there were at least six farmers within 15 miles of his store that used them. He thought it would be impossible to find the chain I needed, but would try. I thought the exercise would be good for him — as well as educational. He called back a few days later to say that he located a manufacturer in central Wisconsin who manufactured a replacement apron chain for the 10A spreader. He was surprised. I wasn't.

Horse-drawn farm machinery can be found at local farm auctions, local farm implement dealers, draft horse auctions, and at manufacturers of new machinery. Appropriate names and addresses can be found in each issue of *The Draft Horse Journal, The Small Farmer's Journal,* or *The Reach.* (See Appendix for details.)

Thirteen years ago Kayo Fraser saw the need for a directory that would help horse people locate the companies and individuals who were providing the equipment, supplies, and services they needed. She started an annual publication called *The Reach, a Horse-in-Harness Directory.* This little publication, now being done by Debbie Evans and Ron Schaaf of Crossville, Tennessee, is invaluable in locating farm machinery, harness, vehicles, and whatever else you may need for your horses.

FORECARTS

Farm machinery designed for tractors can often be adapted for horse use. Perhaps the most useful vehicles on a horse-drawn farm is the forecart — a wheeled vehicle pulled by horses and which, in turn, pulls a piece of farm machinery.

The basic forecart is a seat on a platform over an axle with two wheels. It is pulled

by a team, and then hooked to an implement like a disc, harrow, or two-wheeled spreader. The fore-cart may have hydraulic brakes, but usually doesn't. The first fore-carts were primitive, home-made affairs; now most are newly-manufactured by companies such as Pioneer Equipment of Dalton, Ohio.

Then the three-wheeled fore-cart was developed, with a swivel wheel under the pole to take the weight of the pole, cart, and driver off the necks of the horses. The first time I saw this was in a 1979 *Small Farmer's Journal* article written by Lynn Miller. I took the plans fto my son, Peter, and asked

Lois Winter Photo

him to make one in his welding shop. This cart also featured a high seat, making it easier to see the horses when you were driving two (or more) rows of horses. Some of the more elaborate forecarts of this type also had an engine mounted on the platform. The engine drove a power-takeoff which, in turn, could operate a power-takeoff-driven machine such as a combine or baler.

Next Elmo Reed of Benton, Kentucky designed and built his Three Point Hitch Cart. This horse-drawn three-wheeled cart incorporates a hydraulically controlled 3-point hitch system designed to hook up to and pull any standard catagory 1, 3-point tractor implement. The cart also has a ground-driven power-take-off (PTO) for operating small PTO driven implements such as a mower, hay rake, plow, or manure spreader.

Three views of a John Deere cultivator. First we see it before and after being restored by Craig Winter of Minneota, Minnesota. Craig is one of many individuals who restore old farm machinery. Much of this restored equipment can be found at draft horse auctions. Then we see it being used by Scott Gottschalk, Hutchinson, Minnesota, to cultivate his corn — with a little help from Scott's sorrel mules.

Carla Hammill Photo

Doug Hammill and his four Clydesdales pull a 3-wheeled forecart hooked to a John Deere combine. The combine is powered by a water-cooled John Deere 2-cycle engine — the reel is ground-driven. With Doug is Adam Funk.

The most recent development in the evolution of forecarts is the Teamster 2000, a much larger and heavier 3-wheel forecart which incorporates electric hydraulics (including brakes), a dual power, category I, 3-point hitch, and a ground-driven PTO. The Teamster 2000 is a very well-designed machine and is acclaimed by all who have tried it, including many in the Amish community. Baron Tayler, the designer and manufacturer of the Teamster 2000, is so pleased with the comments he has received from his satisfied customers that he is now offering a 30 day, money-back guarantee on new sales — a remarkable offer which expresses his confidence in the machine.

Two Teamster 2000 Forecarts loaded on a trailer, on their way to new customers. The one in the foreground is equipped with the optional second seat, while the other has one seat.

Baron Tayler Photo

HORSE DRAWN VEHICLES

Horse-drawn vehicles are found in the same way that farm equipment is found. Draft Horse auctions often have a wide selection of vehicles, from those badly in need of repair to those which are brand new. A recent Waverly sale included an unusual buggy with detachable sled runners, four hearses, 6 vis-a-vis, a dozen hitch wagons, over 50 sleighs & cutters, and buggies of all sizes, shapes, and condition.

Again, *The Reach* has 50 listings under the heading "Horsedrawn Vehicles". The current popularity of carriage rides has created a demand for the vis-a-vis type of carriage, and new ones are available in either wood, steel, or fiberglass construction. There are a dozen or so full-time manufacturers of show hitch wagons. Other shops specialize in brand-new reproductions of buggies of all types.

Chuck Carlson of Princeton, Minnesota, advertising his team of mules and hearse by parading them around the Waverly Sale grounds. The hearse later sold to Dale Stevenson of Miles City, Montana, for $5,600. The mules brought $2,350 each, but Chuck "no-saled" them.

Tom Boelz of Clear Lake, Minnesota, built this reproduction of a bobsled that was used on the streets of Duluth back in 1912. Tom had no plans to guide him, but based the new sled on a photo he found the book Heroes in Harness, *by Philip Weber and published by us. What is even more amazing, the new sled was built in just one week, in the middle of winter, to get ready for a horse-logging demonstration Tom put on in St. Paul in February, 1992.*

Robert Tuttle Photo

Dick Hoover of North East, Pennsylvania, built this wagon and then used it to transport the bridal party for their daughter, Wendy's, wedding. The bride and groom traveled ahead in a horse-drawn carriage. Max Manwaring is driving the wagon. A similar trolley wagon is manufactured by the Peltz Manufacturing Company of St. Martin, Minnesota.

HORSESHOES AND HORSESHOEING

Shoes for draft horses are readily available, but farriers are less so. If you can find a farrier who is willing and able to shoe draft horses you should consider yourself fortunate, and do whatever is necessary to keep him happy. Shoeing draft horses is hard, hard, hard work, and most farriers won't do it.

If you have a farrier he will probably have his own shoes. Most draft farriers make their own shoes, or they shape blanks they purchase from a horseshoe company. Anvil Brand Shoe Co. is one of several that manufacture draft shoe blanks (as well as the finished shoes). John Clouden, owner of Anvil Brand, sets up his trailer full of shoes and farrier supplies at the Waverly, Topeka, and Columbus sales, as well as several of the larger draft horse shows. Draft shoes are now being made with rubber pads for horses that spend their days walking on streets or other hard surfaces.

Shoeing stocks are frames of wood or metal used to restrain a draft horse during the shoeing operation, and to tie up the foot being shod. For most shoeing it is easier not to use a stock, as the frame tends to be in the way, particularly if you don't use it constantly. But for horses that are difficult to shoe they are helpful.

It is important that anyone with draft horses be able to trim

Will Lent of Shelby, Michigan, is a professional farrier who specializes in draft shoeing. Here he is shoeing one of the late Elmer Smith's Belgian mares, Julie. Elmer (at Julie's head) was tragically killed in an automobile accident on the way home from the Michigan Great Lakes International Show in 1989.

George Graff Photo

and shoe their own horses — or have someone in the family or nearby who is able and willing to do so. Draft shoes have a tendency to come off, especially the show shoes that are often larger than the foot on which they are nailed. The farrier cannot be expected to come back to tighten a shoe, trim a split hoof, or remove a shoe which is falling off; these are chores that must be done by the owner, as the need arises.

HARNESS

Many people are surprised to learn that harness-making is alive and well, and that harness makers have, as a group, more work than they can handle. There are 48 separate listings in the 1991 issue of *The Reach* under the catagories of Harness and of Harness/Synthetic. All of these listings aren't harness makers to be sure — some are retailers — but there are also many harness makers not listed. I have yet to talk to a harness maker who didn't wish he had a little less work ahead of him.

Another shoeing stock from Christ Miller being loaded on a customer's pickup. Christ and his son brought eight of their stocks from their home in Sugarcreek, Ohio, to the Dixie Draft Horse and Mule Sale to sell as privately (not in the auction) — and all were sold by the end of the first day.

The high cost of leather in recent years has contributed to the development of harness made from synthetic materials. We now see harness made of Biothane, Nylon, and Polypropylene in addition to the traditional leather harness. These synthetic materials are strong, durable and more care-free and lighter-weight than leather. Debbie Evans was one of the pioneers in developing synthetic harnesses from her Deb's Stitch 'n Hitch operation in Crossville, Tennessee. An example of her nylon bridle is shown on page 19 of this book.

SUMMARY

Anyone who really wants to use his draft horses should be able to find all the equipment and vehicles he or she needs. An entire industry has developed to serve the draft horse community.

In 1983 the Meader family of Rochester, New Hampshire, began selling draft horse supplies from a woodshed on their Heritage Farm. Their business grew, and grew — until now the Meader Supply Corporation sells a full line of equipment and supplies for draft horse owners. Their new 42 page catalog lists everything from grooming products to horse trailers, from shoes to shoeing stocks, from harness to manure spreaders, and most things in between. Their obvious success is yet another indication of the health and vigor of the draft horse business.

Synthetic materials are now being used to make some harness instead of leather, reducing costs and weight.

Twin brothers Mike and Steve Bowers are professional horse trainers from Fort Collins, Colorado. Most of the horses they work with are riding horses, but they also train about one team of draft horses each month. In addition they put on Draft Horse Workshops, both at their stables and "on the road". The workshops run for two days, with 15 to 20 participants learning the basics of harnessing, hitching, and driving — both single and double. Here Mike Bowers is bringing a team of Percheron geldings, Chief and Cherokee, back into the barn after doing some hay-hauling chores.

Mark Johnson Photo

Learning How to Use Your Horses

Horsemen aren't born horsemen — they become horsemen after a long period of learning and training. Years ago young people learned to become horsemen from their fathers. They had to, as horses were everywhere, doing everything. Some young people can still learn from family members; but most of us have to find other ways.

As stated earlier, this is not intended as a "how-to-do-it" book. There are other books that do this very well. Instead I will, in this section, attempt to give the reader some ideas on how he or she might learn to harness, hitch, use, and care for his or her draft horses.

The author plowing with three Mischka Farm mares. I didn't do much of this, but wanted to try it. Even trying it wouldn't have been possible without the help and advice of a neighbor, Don Bromeland, who helped me set and adjust the plow. The best way to learn how to use your horses is to have someone show you how.

SELF INSTRUCTION

You can, of course, teach yourself how to use your horses, especially if you have previously raised and worked with riding horses. We trained and broke our own Arabians and Quarter horses to drive, and then later did the same with our draft horses. In the process I read, re-read, and wore out my copies of *The Draft Horse Primer*, the *Work Horse Handbook*, and *Blessed are the Brood Mares*. Books, magazine articles, and pamphlets are a big help if you are going to do it by yourself.

43

Mark Farrell and Karen Lewis learn to drive a team at one of the Horsemanship Schools put on by the Draft Horse & Mule Association. They are using a Pioneer Forecart equipped with dual seats, a very handy arrangement for this purpose.

It also helps to start with a gentle, well-broke horse or team. In this way you are just teaching yourself, not both yourself and the horse.

Talk to people, ask questions. Shortly after having a runaway (everyone has one or more) I mentioned the fact to Dr. Lepird, the Belgian breeder from Esterville, Iowa, as we were visiting at a show. He recommended that I change from the plain snaffle bit I was using — and which is automatically a part of most work bridles — to a buxton bit which has a shank and uses a chain under the chin. This made a lot of sense and was, of course, what we had been using previously with the riding horses. (When draft horses were used all day, everyday, they were tired and the plain snaffle bit worked just fine. But now most horses are overfed and underworked, and more control is often needed.) I have never driven a horse without a buxton bit since, and I have never had another runaway, either. The point is that there is a lot of experience out there, just waiting to be tapped by asking a question. Most draft horse people are friendly folks, very willing to help. But they, like most people, are put off by someone who feels he knows everything, and who won't take any advice.

If you have someone in your area who knows draft horses, and how to use them, by all means take advantage of that situation. People with draft horse knowledge are scarce, and becoming scarcer. They should be treated as a precious resource, which is exactly what they are.

DRAFT HORSE SCHOOLS

In 1980 Maury Telleen, Editor of *The Draft Horse Journal*, decided to revive the Draft Horse and Mule Association, an organization which had ceased to function in the 1950s. I am proud to be one of the founding members, with Membership Certificate Number 50 — which just means I jumped on the bandwagon early, not that I had anything to do with its founding.

One of the missions of the DH&MA is to act as the "educational arm of the heavy horse and mule industry". They do this by publishing educational bulletins and by sponsoring draft horse tours, judging confer-

conferences, and horsemanship schools. The educational bulletins are very helpful; for a listing of what is available you should contact the Association (see the Appendix). Better yet, you should invest $10 and become a member — they will then automatically send you information on their publications and activities.

The tours and the judging conferences are also learning experiences. The tours consist of weeklong trips through a specific area packed with visits to farms and businesses involved with draft horses. The judging conferences are usually two-day events wherein the attendees learn the good and not-so-good points of specific draft horses and mules.

One of the first activities of the re-born Association was to hold a horsemanship school. These week-long schools are still being held, several each year, and are now split between Basic Horsemanship and Advanced Horsemanship. During these schools the students are taught draft horse horsemanship, using a hands-on approach. In other words, the students are soon doing their own harnessing, hitching, and driving of draft horses.

In addition to the schools conducted by the DH&MA and, in some cases, because of the DH&MA leadership in this area, there are now dozens of other draft horse schools and seminars held throughout the country. I counted more than 10 such schools either mentioned or advertised in a recent issue of the *Draft Horse Journal.*

Each year Ron Schaaf and Debbie Evans conduct several week-long draft horse schools at their farm in Crossville, Tenneesee, called Work Horse Weeks. Class-size is limited to just six students. The students stay with Ron and Debbie at their home for the entire week, day and night, learning to use the Suffolk horses raised on the farm. Keeping the students together for 24 hours a day makes for a very intensive draft horse experience. The day's activities are recorded on video tape, with the tapes providing the focus for evening discussions. The cost of the school includes food and lodging for the week. This is just one approach to draft horse schools, but it is one that seems to work out well for Ron and Debbie — and for their students.

Miriam Dunlap takes her turn driving a pair of Farrellawn Clyde geldings at a Draft Horse & Mule Association Horsemanship school. Another student, Alan Shank, sits in the box awaiting his turn with the lines. The teacher, Barry Farrell, is a life-long Clydesdale breeder who was, for many years, head herdsman at the Anheuser-Busch (Budweiser) breeding farm.

Sandee Sage learns to drive four abreast hooked to a disc at one of the Draft Horse Weeks put on each summer by Ron Schaaf and Debbie Evans at their farm in Crossville, Tennessee. These are Suffolk horses, and the right-hand (off-side) horse is their stallion, Ironside Dogwood ("Woody") — the rest are mares.

Tim Christopher and his father, Larry, both of Decorah, Iowa, are professional mule trainers. Mule training is different from horse training. A horse knows who's boss, and it's important that it be you, not he. This approach is counter-productive with mules. With mules it is more a case of mutual appreciation.

PROFESSIONAL TRAINERS

Many draft horses are sent to people who make a business of breaking and training them. If there are Amish farmers in your area there are probably some who will work your horse for a monthly fee. Sometimes all a horse needs is some tough, hard work over an extended period of time for him to settle down and become more useful. There often is more work for a horse to do on an Amish farm than on the horse-

Nancy Christopher Photo

46

owner's suburban lot or hobby farm. Or it might just be that the owner isn't able to spend the "quality time" with his horse that is needed. Whatever the reason, it is often good for a horse to spend some time working on an Amish (or other horse-powered) farm — and many such horse-powered farms are willing to work your horses, along with theirs, for a monthly fee.

There are many people who make a living by buying young colts which catch their eye, then break and train them, and then sell them. Some of these horsemen bring new, matched teams back to the same auction, year after year. As they do this they gain a reputation as a source for good broke teams — and their horses sell at a premium. Richard Hennen of Shakopee, Minnesota, does this, often topping the gelding part of the Waverly Sale with his beautiful matched teams of Percheron or Belgian geldings. People who do this type of work will often take horses owned by others for training or corrective work.

Cathy Zahm of Huntington, Indiana has established an outstanding, well-deserved reputation for breaking, training, and fitting (getting them ready for a show or sale) draft horses. She bought her first draft horse in 1979, after a background in riding horses. In 1990 she trained 62 draft horses, and fitted another 39 drafts for sale. Cathy is a real professional, with a definite plan for breaking horses, and the facilities, equipment, and know-how to get the job done.

Sharon Dean Photo

Cathy Zahm, a professional horse trainer from Huntington, Indiana, working a pair of horses on her breaking sled. The Belgian is her breaking horse, Doc. The Clyde is the horse being schooled, a 2 year-old gelding named Thunder, owned by Bill and Sharon Dean of Ortonville, Michigan.

Many draft horses are "farmed out" to an Amish or other horse-powered farm to work. A period of steady work is good for draft horses, and can change a nervous, high-strung horse into one that is steady and responsive. Too little work is just as much a problem today for draft horses as too much work may have been years ago.

47

Cutting and binding oats near Arthur, Illinois, with, from the teamster's right, Bill, Dolly, Ben, and Dan. Dolly, the only mare in the group, is the mother of the two outside geldings. The owner of this beautiful team is of the Amish faith, and therefore did not want to be pictured or identified. He is proud of his horses, and is pleased to have them shown — and it's fun to see such a happy, alert, well-conditioned, and clean group of horses at work.

Working with Horses — On the Farm

The largest single use for draft horses (and mules) today is on the farm; preparing a seedbed, planting, cultivating, harvesting, and fertilizing. The success and growth of the Amish and Mennonite communities prove that small, diversified livestock farms, powered by horses, are a viable alternative. An entire infrastructure has evolved to support horse-farming, with the machinery and knowledge necessary for this way of life.

People who farm with horses have to pace their work, recognizing the horses' need to rest both during the day and at the end of the day (or half-day). It is ironic that today's "modern" farmer, whose tractor has lights and therefore can run 24 hours a day, has less free time than did his grandfather.

Many thousands of "modern" farmers also have draft horses which are used for certain farm jobs. These horses are often also used for parades, hayrides, wagon trains, horse-pulls, and showing, providing recreation or an extra source of income for the farm family.

Tommy Shoup of Middlebury, Indiana, harrowing his field with three Percheron mares. He unhooked one mare and went off to finish with just a pair to get closer to the fence-line.

49

SEEDBED PREPARATION

Spring is a time of re-birth and hope, as new foals arrive and the ground awakes after its winter rest — and the time to prepare the land for planting.

Plowing is a farm job which horses do well. If the plow is sharp and adjusted properly, and if you use enough horses for the size of the plow and number of shares, it is an enjoyable experience for the teamster and the horses. And it is so quiet, particularly when contrasted with the noise of a diesel tractor at full throttle. There is the jangle of the trace chains on the harness, the popping of the alfalfa roots as they are cut by the plow, and the cries of the birds as they circle around you, picking up the insects from the freshly turned sod.

Discing a freshly plowed field is harder on horses due to the rough surface over which they must walk. But it is a good job for a young horse when hitched with several older ones, and after the first pass the surface is much firmer.

Harrowing and dragging, both before and after planting, are jobs well suited for horses.

So let's go see how some folks do it.

Alvin Miller of Topeka, Indiana uses four Percherons for plowing, one in the furrow and three on the land. He is driving the two near-side (left-hand) horses, and using jockey sticks to control the two off-side horses.

Uwe Schulz of Miles, Iowa, plowing with Denver Traum's six Belgians at a work day held at the farm of Gail Deets, Millidgeville, Illinois. Denver's team includes mares, geldings, and a stallion.

Sam Kissler Photo

Mike Kimzey uses a reversible plow pulled by his Belgian/Shire cross geldings, Bob & Mack, on this five acre field. This is recreation for Mike, as the farm on which he lives and works is a tractor-powered 1800 acre wheat and barley farm near Endicott, Washington. Mike uses his horses for hayrides, local horse-farming demonstrations, and other "change-of-pace" activities.

Heather Erskine Photo

John Erskine of Monroe, Washington, plowing with a team of Shire Geldings. The furrow horse, belonging to Dale Henrickson, was being broke to the plow. John and his wife, Heather, have been raising purebred Shires for 20 years, and enjoy participating in field events, shows, and giving hayrides, as well as using their horses (and those visiting for schooling) for daily farm chores.

Geoffrey Morton has, more than anyone else, kept horse-farming alive and well in England. He now opens his farm to the public on a scheduled basis, and holds courses in horse-farming and logging. Here he is driving eight mares, seven Shires and one Clyde, hooked to two cultivators pulled side by side at his farm near York, England. He has been named a Member of the Order of the British Empire by the Queen for his services to British agriculture. Goeff is a modest man who gives much credit for his success with big hitches like this to Dick Koltz of Greenleaf, Wisconsin. Twenty years ago Dick just happened to meet Goeff at a show in England while Dick was there on a Draft Horse Journal *tour. As a result of some comments Goeff made about a lack of horse equipment Dick sent a gang plow and a booklet showing how to use bigger hitches back to England when he returned to Wisconsin. Without this encouragement Geoff says he might have given up on horse-farming.*

John Colby of Eagle, Wisconsin, plowing a garden with Molly and Dolly, his team of bay Percheron mares.

Justin Mischka on an eight foot John Deere disc pulled by four Percheron mares — more horsepower than was required, but they needed some work.

If the plow is set properly, and the horses are well broke, it's relatively easy to walk behind a walking plow. Diane Coen of Luck, Wisconsin, walked behind her plow for several hours at a field day sponsored by the Wisconsin Draft Horse & Mule Association without any problem.

Karen Forrest Photo

Joe St. Germain of Ladysmith, British Columbia, with a team of 4 & 5 year old Percheron geldings (Ben & Rex) at the Chilliwack, B.C. Plowing Match. The team was completely green when Joe bought them the previous September — it's obvious they have had plenty of practice doing this at home.

Don Bales plowing on his farm near Sabula, Iowa, with three mules on a 14" John Deere sulky plow. The right hand (furrow) mule is Clyde, a 7 year old horse mule. In the center is a 3 year old horse mule that is just learning to work. On the left side, keeping a wary eye on the camera, is Bonnie, a 7 year old mare mule. Bonnie & Clyde were born on the same day, and were always together until Bonnie's untimely death from colic in 1991.

Six Belgians pulling a two-bottom plow in La Grange County, Indiana. The field is being plowed on all four sides. The left-hand leader is beginning to anticipate the turn, and is holding back a bit. All six horses will move onto the plowed land, then swing to their left and start plowing again.

Merle Bannwart of LaPorte, Indiana, plowing with a 16" Emerson plow pulled by his three grey Percheron mares — Halley, Sue, & Nellie. These mares exhibit a femininity about their heads that is very appealing. Each mare had nursing foals at the time this photo was taken.

Clarence Nordstrom of Pine City, Minnesota, plowing with nine Belgians on a 3 bottom John Deere gang plow. Clarence, who is now 77 years old, has been a farmer in Pine City all his life, and still does most of the work on his 240 acre farm with thirteen head of Belgian horses. All but two of the nine horses in this picture were raised by Clarence.

Sue Brennan Photo

Bob Brennan plowing on his farm near Hillsdale, New York, with four Percheron geldings. The outside horses are called Jack and Bob — the two on the inside are Mack 'n Tosh. The Rooster, LeRoy, think it's great fun, picking up the bugs and grubs being exposed by the plowing. Bob does enough horse-farming on his 300 acre farm so that when he competes in the local plowing matches he usually comes home with at least one first prize.

Lonnie Yoder, age 14, is "packing corn" with a double roll packer on his father's farm in La Grange County, Indiana. The left horse, Sam, is a roan color, once very common and now pretty well bred out of the American Belgian, but still remembered fondly by the old-timers.

Don Bromeland, Elkhorn, Wisconsin, plowing some heavy clay soil with a one-bottom Emerson sulky plow. The left (near) horse is a two-year old gelding called Dick owned by Dennis Garoutte, also of Elkhorn. The other two, Billy & Jerry, are seven year-olds owned by Don. The evener is set over 1" so that each of the two older horses must pull more of the load than the younger horse.

A six-abreast of mules pulling a large disc for Linus Loeffelholz of New Glarus, Wisconsin.

Walt Becker of Hillsdale, Wisconsin uses an unusual two-bottom Huntsmen plow behind his four Percheron geldings. The plow was manufactured in 1918 by Herb Huntsmen of Long Prairie, Minnesota. The plow's wheels are six feet apart, making it possible to hitch two horses on each side of the pole without having the near horse walking on plowed ground. It was called a "rock plow" since each plowshare is individually attached to the frame with a universal joint-like connection, and can move up, down, or to either side as rocks are encountered. This feature, along with a very low center of gravity, makes it virtually impossible to tip over. (Oh yes, a conventional sulky plow will tip over quite easily if it hits a rock just right.)

Robert Hogg, Sr. of Mecosta, Michigan, harrowing his paddock with, from his left, Dolly, Dan, Jule, and Abe. Bob and his daughter, Beth, use their nine Belgians for plowing, raking, harrowing, spreading, and hay-rides.

Nancy Hogg Photo

Camey Thompson Photo

Steve Thompson of the Circle T Ranch near Castro Valley, California, seeding oats with an end-gate seeder on a farm wagon pulled by four Belgians. Steve's helper, Keith Thomas, keeps the hopper for the broadcast seeder full as they travel back and forth in the field.

PLANTING

Planting is a job horses can do well. The planter usually rolls on wheels, making it relatively easy to pull. The seedbed is well-worked and firm, and easy for the horses to walk on. The horses get an automatic rest whenever it is necessary to stop and add more seed. The main challenge, especially with row crops like corn, is to make a straight row; in most cases your neighbor will be able to check how straight your rows are after the crop comes up.

Rick Maage of Hardin, Montana, planting corn with his 15.1 hand Belgian mules, Kate & Nel. Rick is a veternarian who uses his mules mostly for recreation. Here he is working in an irrigated field north of Hardin.

Deb Maage Photo

Jean Kuehl Photo

Dennis Kuehl seeding oats and grass at his Mountain View farm near Loveland, Colorado. Dennis is using a McSherry grain drill with patent dates from 1864 to 1871 — a lovely piece which his wife, Jean, would love to display in their living room. They have about a dozen registered Belgians which they use for farm work and for show — a welcome break from their work as full-time educators.

Dave Stalheim gives his son, Justin, a driving lesson while he demonstrates at a Field Day sponsored by the Wisconsin Draft Horse & Mule Association. Dave is a dairy farmer from Amery, Wisconsin, who also raises Clydesdales.

A four-row corn planter pulled by four Belgians. On the driver's right is Queen, then her son, Jim, then the geldings Bob & Kit. The photo was taken near LaGrange, Indiana, where most of the farming is done with horses.

Bob Donley of Middletown, California, seeding red oat hay with his team of Belgian geldings, King and Mike. The seeder is a 6 foot Van Brunt / John Deere made in the early 1900s. Bob enjoys taking his horses on wagon trains, using them for 4-H and other children-related activities, and for some farming. He is a Director in the local county fair, and was instrumental in getting a draft horse show started there.

Sharon Eide Photo

Eddie Durmon of Vivian, Louisiana, with Dolly and Molly, two grade Belgian mares, preparing garden rows for planting. Eddie is knocking the top of the rows off, covering any tiny weeds that have grown up since the rows were made. Later he will plant peas, corn, potatoes, okra, tomatoes, cucumbers, and peppers in the water furrow. The Durmons raise Belgians, using them mostly for recreational purposes such as parades, hayrides, Christmas caroling, and giving children rides.

Rita Durmon Photo

Bobby Chaffin Photo

Dorn Wise laying off corn rows on his farm near Pulaski, Tennessee. After the rows are marked he follows with a single-row corn planter. Dorn prefers the single-row planter over a two-row planter because of the steep hillsides on his farm. The horses are registered Percheron mares.

It's springtime in New Liskeard, Ontario, and Paul St. Onge, age 73, is marking garden rows with the Belgian mare, SLF Dolly Farceur. John St. Onge, owner of the mare, is hidden behind the horse, handling the lines.

Claire St Onge Photo

Ken Stapes planting corn with the two and three year old geldings, Dick & Dan. Ken uses this team for haying, hauling manure, skidding logs, and other chores around their farm neaer Stanley, New York.

Earl Holdren Photo

One boy rides and guides the mule while his cousin cultivates the garden.

Jerry Irwin Photo

CULTIVATING

Cultivating is also a job well suited for horse-power. The slow pace of the horse makes it easier to do a more thorough job of weed removal. And if cultivating is weed removal, we can also include spraying for weeds in this catagory. There are ground-driven sprayers available for those who wish to spray weeds, or the PTO equipped forecarts discussed previously could be used to power a sprayer.

Shelby McGinn Photo

Ed McGinn enjoys "working in God's good earth", raising corn, beans, and watermelons with the help of his 900 pound, 12 yr old mare mule, Pepper. Ed and Pepper live near Monroe, North Carolina.

Billy Norvell cultivating tobacco with two 2-yr olds, Smokey (a stallion) and Daisey (a filly). Billy raises hay, tobacco, corn, and cattle on his 170 acre farm near Danville, Kentucky.

Lisa Norvell Photo

Lloyd Nelson weeding his corn with a four-horse, two-row International cultivator at his farm near Fergus Falls, Minnesota. Lloyd and his son, Bruce, milk 45 cows and farm 400 acres, using horses for many of their farm chores.

Dorothy Nelson Photo

Bonnie Nance Photo

Bobby Pinkston of Hartford, Kentucky dusting tobacco with his Belgian gelding, Prince. The burlap on the horse's back and the netting on the bridle are both to help ward off the horseflies.

Cultivating a vegetable crop in Holmes County, Ohio. The young man is able to steer the cultivator with his feet, making the steering of the horses not quite as important — they just seem to move along by themselves, allowing the teamster to concentrate on the location of the cultivator shoes.

Judy Wolf Photo

Richard Wolf of Attica, New York, seems to be adrift in his field of corn as he does his cultivating with Ben and Barney, a pair of Belgian geldings who were also pictured on page 4.

Spraying corn ground with a herbicide from a ground-driven sprayer on a farm in northern Indiana.

Bud Walsh Photo

Lawrence Starck tosses an oat bundle to his son, Greg, while George Hulse drives the team, a pair of registered mares, Columbine Bess and Columbine Shirley, owned by Lawrence. The horses are protected from the flies by fly-nets over their harness and ribbons on the brow band of their bridles. The Starcks are from Berthoud, Colorado, and this action took place at a Field Day on the Dennis Speicher farm, also of Berthoud.

GRAIN HARVESTING

Grain-binding, both for small grains and for corn, is a thing of the past in most areas of the midwest, and we are the poorer for its absence. Leaving the straw, chaff, cornstalks and corn-cobs, and some of the grain itself in the field is a poor substitute for using it in the barn for animal feed or bedding, and hauling it back out to the field as manure. Is there a sight on a diversified farm more beautiful and satisfying than a field of shocked grain bundles?

During my high school years we lived in a house (not a farm) in the country, and our next-door neighbor was Leo Yanney, a dairy farmer. One of my duties was to walk to his barn each evening and get a small pail of milk. I would come home with my clothes well saturated with the smell of the cowbarn after standing around for a half-hour or so, watching Leo milk his cows. Leo kept a team of black workhorses which he used for many farm chores. He had a steel-wheeled Farmall 10-20 tractor which he used for plowing, belt-power, and some of the harder jobs, but he preferred to use his horses for other tasks. He also owned a Case threshing machine — again the last in the area. Leo vowed to bind and thresh his oats as long as he was able to buy binder twine. He retired from farming before binder twine became unavailable, as that day has not yet come.

Laverne McMahon of Birch Hills, Saskatchewan, with his registered Percheron mares, Prideway Lady Ann and Prideway Karen Lou. The six month filly foal has not yet been weaned, and is tied to her mother. Laverne shows his horses at the local fairs, as well as cultivating, seeding, grain-binding, and bringing in the bundles — all done for demonstrations in their area.

Jean McMahon Photo

Tom Sadler Photo

Bringing in the wheat sheaves (bundles) on the Ian Sadler farm outside Strathmore, Alberta. A four-horse team pulls the stook loader (shock loader) which conveys the wheat sheaves up onto the wagon, eliminating the need to toss them up by hand. Another team pulls the wagon while it is being loaded, and then takes it to the waiting threshing machine.

Jerry Irwin Photo

Picking corn on a farm in Lancaster County,
Pennsylvania. The gasoline-engine powered
corn picker is pulled by a mixed team of Belgian
and Percheron geldings, and the farm wagon
collecting the corn is pulled by a team of mules.

One of my most vivid childhood memories is threshing day at the Leo Yanney farm. The neighbors all came to help, bringing more food than could possibly be eaten — but we tried our best. I remember the horses bringing in the bundles, and the chaff blowing down my neck as I climbed onto the threshing machine to crank the blower pipe to a new position. This is a scene out of the history books for most of us, but for many it is still it's the only way to harvest small grains. Those who are still doing it this way probably don't think of it in this romantic, pleasant way. One of the tragedies of life is that today is the "good old day" of tomorrow, but that we often don't recognize it as such until tomorrow.

A scene of contrasts near Arcola, Illinois. A boy drives his pony, Cindy, out to the field carrying a water bucket with a drink for his father. In the background you can see a modern grain elevator complex. The farmer stops his work every three rounds to give the team a rest and to brush the gears on the binder with a heavy oil; a distinct contrast from the go-for-broke attitude of most combining operations today.

Evelyn Hanson Photo

A handsome team helps themselves to a bit of lunch while the teamster is elsewhere, doing the same.

Threshing oats at the Merle Fischer farm near Jefferson, Wisconsin. The Percheron geldings stand patiently while Daren Fischer and Mark Jordan toss oat bundles from the wagon onto the thresher conveyor. Wayne Randall adjusts the direction of the straw blower pipe, and the threshed oats are augered into a gravity box wagon. In 1990 Merle worked the ground and then planted, cut, and threshed the oats from 50 acres, all with his Percherons providing the power.

Gib Brenner drives a 27-mule team pulling a hillside combine on the Don Thomas Ranch near Waitsburg, Washington. The mules are hitched in four rows of six each, with three mules out in the lead. The lead mules are 50' from the driver, who sits on an elevated perch. The combine is powered by a gasoline engine, and the grain header cuts a 16' swath. It is called a hillside combine because the downhill wheel is cranked down to keep the threshing floor inside the combine level. The mules were provided by Don Thomas, Ed Robinson, Gib Brenner, and Dick Durham.

Walt Becker of Hillsdale, Wisconsin, binding corn with a McCormick Deering binder pulled by his 8 and 11 year-old black Percheron geldings.

Catherine Tyler Photo, Driving Digest Magazine

Joe Mischka Photo

HAYMAKING

Farm haymaking (as opposed to ranch haymaking) has been changed by the introduction of the crimper, a device that requires a power-take-off (PTO) to operate. The crimper, or conditioner, eliminates at least one day of drying time — often making the difference between hay that is excellent quality and hay that is rained on, and of much poorer quality. The mower-conditioner, which both cuts and crimps the hay in one operation, requires a substantial source of power to operate. The most common way to power a horse-drawn mower-conditioner, or haybine, is with a gasoline engine mounted on the implement, or with a gasoline-driven engine on a forecart. It is also possible to use a modern forecart, like the Forecart 2000, with a ground-driven PTO. The same approaches can be used to power a hay baler.

Raking hay is an excellent job for horses, especially for those who don't get enough work on a regular basis to be really toughened up. The drag on the horses is nice and steady, the footing excellent, and the weather ususally pleasant.

The Coen family mowing hay on their farm near Luck, Wisconsin. Diane is in front, followed by her husband, Bruce, followed by Bruce's father, Mark. They are using #9 and #7 International mowers. The horses are also related. Bruce is driving a mother and her son, and the other four horses (all mares) are also daughters or grand-daughters of that same mare.

75

Dale Friends photo

A. Jack Fuller mowing hay on his farm near Tioga, Pennsylvania. His team consists of a stallion named Ben (on the off-side) and a mare called Kate. Jack has now moved to Middlebury Center, Pennsylvania, and he took his Percheron horses with him. He has been working with draft horses since he was 7, and is still finding new things to do with them. Several years ago he started a bobsled festival at his farm — last year this festival attracted 4,000 people for a horse-drawn ride in the snow.

Tim Christopher mowing hay with a team of mules on his farm near Decorah, Iowa. Tim does all his farming with mules — some are his and some are there for training.

Nancy Christopher Photo

Raking alfalfa hay with a team of registered Belgian mares north of New Haven, Indiana, another area where most of the farming is done with horses.

Bob White of Stitzer, Wisconsin, mowing hay with his team of Percheron geldings, Tim and Tom. Bob cuts, rakes, and stacks 25 acres of hay with this team each year.

Joe Mischka Photo

These young folks are loading mint in northern Indiana. Hay is loaded in the same manner, with the loader trailing the wagon and the hay (or mint) picked up and pushed up the ramp and onto the back of the wagon.

Charles Lent of Purchase, New York, raking hay with his team of Belgians, Vic and George.

Barbara Lent Photo

Jelane McNish Photo

Harold McNish of Midddlefield, Ohio, uses a gasoline engine to power his horse-drawn baler as Jim Meyer stacks the bales on the wagon. The team consists of a mare, Penny, and a gelding, Bob. Harold enjoys using his horses for plowing, haying, spreading manure, and other farm chores.

Bonnie Nance Photo

The baling is done with four horses pulling a ground-driven baler on the Victor Lengacher farm near Montgomery, Indiana. A large bull wheel provides the power to operate the baler. The two inside horses are being driven, and the two outside horses are controlled with jockey sticks.

79

A mixed team pulling an engine-powered haybine in Holmes County, Ohio.

OTHER FARM CHORES

A team of Suffolk geldings are happy to be out in the spring air, and they make the manure fly. This team is owned, and is being driven by, Ron Schaaf of Crossville, Tennessee.

Probably the most common chore which draft horses perform on a farm is hauling out the manure. Even hobby farmers who may not raise many (or any) crops will have manure to haul if they have horses. And let's not kid ourselves, those big horses make a lot of manure. They eat about twice as much as a riding horse, and the natural and inevitable result of this takes lots of hauling.

Many farmers with tractors find it more convenient to haul manure with their horses than with the tractor. If your chores involve frequent stops to pick up the manure, as with stalls or a gutter on both sides of a barn driveway, you save lots of climbing up on and down off the tractor when you use a team, and just have to pick up the lines.

In addition to manure spreading, horses are called upon to do a wide variety of farm chores. The following page illustrate some of the less common activities.

Lori Phelps Photo

Nellie Howe of Guilford, Vermont, collecting maple sap with Duke and Bell. Nellie died suddenly in August, 1991, after a lifetime of working with horses. She and H. Stubby Howe were married in 1939, and they worked together everyday until her death. Nellie was always the teamster — her first job was digging out holes for basements with horses and a scoop. She went on to log and farm with her horses, and at one time collected maple sap from a 1,000 bucket sugar bush.

Andre' Coulombe Photo

William Delaney is removing a sap bucket from the Maple tree, and will pour the sap into the tub on the bobsled. His son, Jody, is driving their team, Dan and Don, a pair of seven year-old Belgian geldings. The Delaney's, from Kingsbury, Quebec, show their Belgian hitch at many fairs throughout Quebec each summer.

Louis Chavez Photo

An early September morning finds Tony Williams harvesting potatoes from the 5-10 acres raised each year on the S & K Farm, a community of 100 Christians who make their living on 600 acres near Delta Junction, Alaska. Tony is head teamster, keeping between 10 to 20 draft horses, with several teams hitched each day for the farming and logging activities at the farm. They use horsepower to cut, rake, and haul the hay from 200 acres and to bind and thresh 50-60 acres of oats and barley, using a tractor just for baling. In September their harvest of moose, caribou, and grizzley is hauled down from the mountains with their draft horses. Tony believes their homesteading way of life would be impossible without their draft horses.

T. R. Dean is bringing 1600# of hand-picked cotton from the Houston Northen farm near Belton, Texas to the Vandiver Gin at Moody Texas. This 1600# of seed cotton (the work of 5 men for one day) will yield about 500# of lint cotton. The Peter Schuttler wagon was sold by the Smith & Peyton hardware store, and purchased by Mr. Northen in 1923. Riding with Mr. Dean is Mr. Northen's son, Maurice.

Clois D. Stone Photo

Nancy Hunt Photo

Ivan Thornburg and Joe Hines are pressing sorghum at the Sherman Hunt farm near Winchester, Indiana. Sorghum is planted in early May, at the same time corn is planted. Before first frost the leaves are stripped by hand. The remaining stalks are cut, hauled to the press, and beheaded. Then the stalks are fed into the horse-driven press, with the juice dropping into a bucket. The juice is then cooked over a fire for 4 to 6 hours until it thickens and becomes sorghum molasses. It takes 7-10 gallons of juice to make one gallon of molasses. The molasses is used for cooking, and the spent stalks are fed to cows and pigs.

Saundra Bogart Photo

Horsepower to the rescue at the Harry Bogart farm near Bronaugh, Missouri. In addition to pulling out stuck tractors Harry likes to use his horses for some farm work and for pleasure drives.

Walter Fuez of Moran, Wyoming, feeding hay to the 400 cows on his ranch near Yellowstone Park. The team keeps the sled moving as the loose hay is forked off the side. Walter was in his 70s when these pictures were taken, and he was still feeding his cows in this same manner for 180 days each year. Walt and his wife, Betty, are now retired, but their daughter, Chris, and her husband, Jerome, now operate the Fuez Ranch. The wheel team, Pat and Mike, are Percherons; the leaders, Mack and Turk, are part Shire.

Working with Horses —
At the Ranch

There's a difference between a farm and a ranch — but I'm not sure what it is. Perhaps it used to be that farms involved more fencing and fewer acres than a ranch. But now, with fences torn out on the very large farms I suspect that this difference may have blurred. Maybe farms involve plowing and/or planting, and ranches don't, but here too I see exceptions as some large wheat operations are referred to, by their owners, as ranches. Whatever the difference, if you refer to a rancher's place as a farm you will quickly be corrected. It reminds me of the song in *Oklahoma* where the playwright pleaded for the farmer and the rancher to be friends.

At any rate, I have tried to separate the ranch activities from the farm activities — but am well aware that this distinction is somewhat arbitrary.

A cage is used to form haystacks at the Haythorn Ranch near Arthur, Nebraska. Four Belgians pull a cable which drags the hay up the inclined ramp where it is dumped into the cage. The horses start, stop, and back-up by voice command. The Haythorn Ranch consists of 90,000 acres (owned and leased) devoted to raising cattle, and has been operated by a member of the Haythorn family since 1884.

HAYMAKING

Ranches are often located in parts of the country where rainfall is scarce, making it possible to store hay outside, either in stacks of bales or in loose piles, rather than inside a barn or shed. Many ranches raise livestock and use draft horses to bring hay to their animals during the winter months. It is only natural for these same ranches to use their horses during the summer months as well for their haymaking.

The scarce rainfall also results in a different type of hay than is grown on midwest or southern farms. Western hay usually consists of grasses, rather than the legumes (alfalfa) grown elsewhere. The number of cuttings is less (often only one per year), and the cut hay is in no danger of being rained on before it is cured or dried. This makes the slower pace of horsedrawn haymaking less of a drawback than it is in a wetter climate.

Another method of making a haystack. Here the horses push the loose hay up the inclined ramp (called a beaverslide) where it is then distributed and packed down by another rancher.

Danny Weaver Photo

Joan Buckles Photo

Buck Buckles moves the hay-stacker to another spot on the Shadbolt Cattle Co. Ranch near Gordon, Nebraska. The six grey Percheron geldings are all half-brothers. During the summer months this ranch stacks 2,500 tons of loose hay to feed their 1,000 cattle during the winter.

Katherine Bond Photo

Lennie Campbell using a hay-sweep to pick up and push the loose hay to the stacker. The Campbell Ranch, in the Hoback Basin near Bondurant, Wyoming, is operated almost entirely with horsepower. Lennie and his brother are the third generation of Campbells on this ranch.

Not all hay is put up loose. Here Von Wilson picks up bales at the Smith Rancho near Hayden, Colorado. The sled, with its low profile, is much easier to load than a wagon. The Belgian geldings, Jake and John, have very little difficulty pulling the loaded sled on the grass-covered meadow.

WINTER FEEDING

Livestock ranches in the western states feed hay to their animals during the winter months when the grass is dormant and the ground is snow-covered. There's no easy way to do this job. Many ranches still feed their livestock (usually cattle) in the winter by bringing hay to them on a bobsled pulled by draft horses. This may seem old-fashioned to some, but to those who have to get the job done it still seems to be the best, and least difficult, way.

Western Horseman photo by Gary Vorhes

Feeding hay is a one-man operation with Greg Ray operating the hydrofork mounted on a sled pulled by four draft horses — three Percherons and one Belgian — in the North Park country of Colorado. The team pulls the sled forward and Greg pitches the hay off the moving sled with the hydrofork.

George Wright Photo

No, the team wasn't walking backwards — they just stopped and turned around to see what they had done. This lovely scene was taken at the George Wright ranch near Caldwell, Idaho. The near-side (left) horse is Hank, age 27. His mate is Ribbon, age 22. George says that they just don't come any better than these two.

89

A mixed draft team and one dog (Belk) wait while Roland Moore piles hay on the wagon with his hydrofork powered by a 16 hp Briggs & Stratton engine. The haystack was made with a beaverslide, and the wagon holds about 1 ton of loose hay. This scene was at Roland's Cold Springs Ranch near Norris, Montana. The Percherons are geldings called Gus and Bo; the Belgians are mares called Vicky and Susan. Crocett Nash is helping Roland.

Buck Buckles bringing hay to the cattle on the Shadbolt Cattle Co. ranch near Gordon, Nebraska. The horses drag the hay on the sled with cables, and the hydrofork is used to pitch it off. The six Percheron geldings are driven with two lines, using jockey sticks to control the four outside horses. This area doesn't get much snow so they don't have to stay on a trail, making the six-abreast a practical arrangement. The horses pretty much drive themselves, listening to Buck's voice commands. The ranch gates are built to accomodate the six-abreast hitch.

Mike Logan Photo

Dan Gill Photo

Bruce Benson and his crew bring a load of hay to the cattle at his ranch near Avon, Montana. Bruce and his brother, Fred, do their ranching in the Little Blackfoot River Valley region of Western Montana.

Otto Jensen returns to the barn at his ranch near Lewistown, Montana, after feeding his cattle.

91

Katherine Bond Photo

Two views of Kevin Campbell at his ranch near Bondurant, Wyoming. At the top his team is peacefully pulling the load of hay through the snow, on their way to feed the cattle. As the snows build up the horses and sled pack down a trail or roadway, and the horses learn to keep on the trail or risk being stuck up to their bellies. After a heavy or deep snowfall the track must be packed down again with just the team (the teamster may walk alongside, driving the team while wearing snowshoes), or with the team and an empty wagon. At the right we see Kevin breaking a trail through the heavy snow with his horses and an empty sled. When the going gets tough, the tough get going.

Arthur Renshaw Photo

Reni Nixon Photo

Cattle aren't the only animals which must be fed during the winter. Don Nixon uses his horses to winter feed 1,000 sheep and 400 cattle on his ranch near Alzada, Montana. The horses in the top picture are full brothers and sister, half Percheron and half Belgian. The bottom pictures shows a team of grade Percherons making large circles in the

pasture pulling a wagon holding a gravity box filled with shell corn. As they make their large circles the corn flows out onto the ground, feeding the ewes their ration of 1/2 pound per day.

Barb Uhrig Photo

Bruce Oliphant bringing hay to his cattle, with the Colorado Rockies in the background. Bruce and Joanna Oliphant raise registered Percheron horses, and use them for a wide variety of chores, on their ranch near Silt, Colorado.

Joanna Oliphant Photo

Cindy Thyme Photo

Ron Stoltenberg of Auburn, Wyoming, feeding his cattle with a team consisting of three Shires and one Percheron (the grey) — and there is always at least one dog supervising the operation.

Bob Klaren feeds elk at the Scab Creek Feedground near Boulder, Wyoming, for the Wyoming Fish and Game Department during the winter, using a team owned by Kevin Campbell (page 92). Bob lives in Pinedale, Wyoming, and during the rest of the year works as a cowboy for the Upper Green River Cattle Association.

Jonita Sommers Photo

Draft Horse Journal Photo

Ron Dean is in charge of 22 State of Wyoming feed grounds where approximately 12,000 elk are fed a supplemental diet of hay throughout the winter. By feeding elk the State attempts to minimize the damage done by them to the nearby rancher's haystacks. Elk feeding starts as soon as the hunting season ends so that they do not scatter out into the mountains, looking for feed. The teamsters doing this work come back year after year, and come to know the elk as individuals, and call them by name.

Don McIntosh skidding logs with his team of Belgian geldings at his ranch near Quesnel, British Columbia. Don uses his horse for logging and other ranch chores, as well as competing in pulling contests during the summer months.

Michael Breuer Photo

Working with Horses — In the Woods

Horse logging covers a wide range of activities, from the full-time professional logger, to the person who does some serious logging for part of the year, most often during the winter, to those who use their horses to drag some firewood out of their own woodlot. In each case horse logging is generally kinder and gentler to the environment than is machine logging. The horses require a narrower trail in which to travel, and they do not tear up the ground as crawler tractors do.

Horses are used in a commercial horse logging operation to skid the fallen trees out of the woods, or to a place within the woods, where they can be loaded on a truck and carried away to the sawmill or processing plant. The days of bringing logs to the riverbank with horses or oxen, and floating them down to the mill, are gone. Mammoth trucks with self-loading hydraulic forks now transport the logs to the mill after the logger has moved them to a spot where the trucker can load.

Logging is a dangerous activity, and horse logging is no less so. It is not something that should be undertaken without some understanding of the hazards involved. The horses used in horse logging must be calm, well-broke, and accustomed to working through voice commands.

Arnold Langmaid of St. Johnsbury, Vermont, bringing out four large logs on the bobsled with two Belgian Mares, Kate and Princess. Arnold and his son, Don, are dairyfarmers who enjoy working with the horses in the woods during the long New England winters.

Duwayne Langmaid Photo

There are about 50 full-time commercial loggers in the United States who use horses either exclusively or significantly in their operations. A Horse Logger's Newsletter has been started by Greg Caudell of Keller, Washington, to help loggers share information about their successes and problems. Neil Bailey of Pinedale, Wyoming, has founded The North American Horse and Mule Loggers Association to do the same kinds of things. These efforts are a little tentative, and their successes are not assured, as they are undertaken by people who have more vision and understanding than they have time and money. Details on both the newsletter and the association are listed in the Appendix.

In addition to these full-time loggers there are literally hundreds of folks who use their horses to skid logs out of the woods on a part-time or casual basis. Frequently they are getting their own firewood, and perhaps a little extra to sell. Others sell their logs commercially, but on a seasonal or part-time basis.

The Baltimore Gas & Electric Company recently hired Paul Yoder, his son, Nathan, and Michael Wheatley, to use horses to remove about 1,000 trees in suburban Baltimore County. This is part of an overall project involving the removal of about 10,000 trees to make room for a new transmission line. The horses will be used in the marshes and wetlands where the crawler-mounted logging equipment would raise havoc with the environment. This is not an isolated example — similar situations are taking place throughout the country. As horses are shown to be useful in these type of situations they will be called upon more and more.

Moni Wender of Iron Mountain, Michigan, is skidding logs out of the woods with Dan and King, a team of Belgian geldings. These are big horses — the wear 30" collars and have a combined weight of 4,500 pounds. Moni is still going strong at age 83, but has now changed to a smaller team which is easier to harness.

Al Cini Photo

Nathan and Elly Foote Photos

Everyone is a little different, but Nathan and Elly Foote are more different than most. In the early 1970s they spent nearly five years making a 20,000 mile trail ride from the southernmost tip of South America to Southbank, British Columbia. That must've been enough travel, for they are still in Southbank where they log with horses and conduct horsemanship schools for girls at their Saddle Tramp Wilderness Ranch. They have produced a video to show how they log with horses. Nathan fells the trees — 200 year old, 90 foot tall spruce — and cuts off the top and branches. Note that Nathan wears a hard had and noise suppressors. The remaining 50 foot long log is skidded down to a landing by Elly where it will be later loaded onto the bed of a large logging truck. The truck will carry 40 to 60 logs, depending on their diameter. The log which Elly is skidding at the right has a butt diameter of about 23", a little large for horse logging without an arch or other aid, but she is bringing it down a very steep trail (about 30%). The optimal skid trail has just a slight incline and is no longer than 300 feet.

Roger Daugherty of Oregon City, Oregon, logging with three greys (one is half Belgian) in the Mount Hood National Forest. Roger has been doing salvage and thinning work for the U. S. Forest Service since 1980. During his peak years, before the spotted owl controversy, he was working 5 teams with 7 loggers. About ten years ago Roger designed and built a four-wheeled logging arch to lift the butt end of the log, making it easier for the horses to skid them. With the arch a pair of horses

can skid logs of 5,500 pounds or more. The four wheels (as opposed to two) eliminate the need for a fixed pole, making it much easier on the horses. With the cut-back in Forest Sevice work during the past five years the Daughertys (Roger, Anne, and Aaron, their 5 year old son) have been developing a cut-your-own Christmas tree operation which they plan to open in 1993, and on which they will use their Percheron horses. They are also ready and eager to resume their logging work as soon as it becomes available again.

Anne Daugherty Photos

Kay Kelly Photo

Ron Cammack of Homedale, Idaho, with a team of 3 and 4 yr-old Belgian geldings (Clyde and Vic), logging post, pole, and firewood material in the Blue Mountain area of eastern Oregon. Back home Ron uses his team for plowing, cattle feeding, hayrides, and hauling Christmas carolers. It takes an agile teamster to keep clear of the log with a team as lively as this one.

Bucky Burroughs Photo

Tony takes a well-deserved drink after pulling out logs all morning for his owner, Bucky Burroughs of Canterbury, Connecticut. Tony, who was 16 years old at the time, helped Bucky pull out over 50 cords of wood for firewood the previous winter. Bucky is a dairyfarmer, milking 90 Holsteins, who uses his horses whenever possible on his farm.

Ross Milne Photo

Grover Edwards of Sault Saint Marie, Ontario, skidding a large log through the snow with his team of Belgian geldings, Bud and Willy. Grover still works in the bush with these two horses 13 years after this photo was taken.

Photo provided by Jason Rutledge

Not all the work in the woods involves log skidding. Jason Rutledge of Copper Hill, Virginia, was hired by the local power company to pull a fiber optic cable through the hills with one of his Suffolk horses. The area was too hilly to use power equipment, and the alternative was to pull the cable by hand. Jason and his horse completed the project several weeks ahead of schedule.

Forrest Davis of Ronan, Montana, drives the lead team and Clancy Swope the wheel team as they skid a 2,700 pound log to the logging truck. This scene took place at one of the many Schools of Driving and Farming which Forrest conducted at the Slack Point Ranch in Polson, Montana.

Jim Cornish of Brunswick, Maine, skidding logs with help from his mares, Molly and Maggie. Jim is clearing a house-site, a job he is frequently called upon to do as the horses disturb the land so much less than does crawler logging equipment. He also provides firewood for a regular clientele, selling an average of 100 cords of firewood each year, and cuts logs for local sawmills, a nearby paper mill, and a sawmill he and his brothers own. Both mares are in foal, and Jim enjoys raising and breaking their colts.

Motor vehicles are not allowed on Mackinac Island, Michigan, making it a unique and delightful tourist location. Here the Grand Hotel omnibus leaves the hotel porch, loaded with guests (inside) and their luggage (on top), on its way to the dock where a ferry will transport them back to the mainland — and to reality. The Grand Hotel, built in 1887, boasts of its 700 foot long veranda. It is open from mid-May through October, and maintains its elegant atmosphere through a dress code that includes the requirement that male guests wear a coat and tie after 6:00 pm.

Working with Horses — Moving People

Central Park in New York City used to be one of the very few places where you would see a horse and carriage. For a few dollars you could ride the carriage through the Park and imagine how it was at the turn of the Century when there were no cars. How this has changed. Now virtually every major city in the United States has at least one carriage ride company. Many smaller cities do also, especially those with a tourist trade.

There also has been a dramatic increase in the number of people who will hire out a carriage and horse(s) for weddings, anniversaries, and other events. Theme parks such as Disneyland move people around the grounds with horse-drawn busses that carry large numbers of people.

Hayrides and sleighrides have become big business. The 1991 Wisconsin Winter Adventures book published by the Wisconsin Tourism Council lists 53 separate sleighride operators in the State of Wisconsin!

The growth of this type of activity has led to the formation of an organization called Carriage Operators of North America (CONA). This group has an annual convention and a periodic newsletter, both of which are intended to further communication and help between teamsters involved in carriage ride businesses. CONA helps new operators get started, answers questions for established operators, and provides a support network when insurance, animal-rights activist, or other problems arise. See the Appendix for details on CONA.

Mrs. LaVern Schulz Photo

Gene Steidinger, Sr., has teamster honors for the wedding of Chris Schulz of Marathon, Wisconsin. The Belgian mare is Jody, grand-daughter of the legendary Marcus Du Marias. Gene has never been without draft horses, using them now mostly for an annual wagon train and other fun activities.

Harold Kinart Photo

Robert Barnes does a wedding in his home town of Sarnia, Ontario. Robert, who is 75 years old, still does many weddings, hayrides and parades, as well as some farm chores with his horses. He is finely attired in a black tuxedo, bow tie, and hat. The yellow flashing light on the top of the surrey is a concession to safety.

Loa Dawn Vincent Photo

Mike Vincent provides the carriage and horses for a wedding in his home town of Carroll, Iowa. Mike has a lively carriage business in the area using four Clydesdale horses. The pictures on these two pages illustrate that many different types of vehicles can be (and are being) used for weddings.

Jim and Sue Kane operate a carriage business in Burlington, Wisconsin. Here they are doing a wedding in the nearby town of Lake Geneva. The white vis-a-vis has become the color of choice of wedding customers, and is used by many carriage operators. White is, however, an inappropriate color from a historical standpoint.

Joe Mischka Photo

The Cheshire Carriage Service, owned by Steve Apted and operated by his son, Dan, provides tours of the St. Louis, Missouri, downtown area as well as wedding and anniversary drives with their fleet of 20 carriages and 14 grey Percheron geldings.

Horses used on the streets in carriage ride operations are often a cross between a draft horse and a riding horse. This colorful horse is one of a group of crossbred horses which work the Milwaukee streets for the Shamrock Carriage Co. owned by Rick Murphy.

A team of Belgian geldings pull an antique buss with a cut-under front wheel design at Greenfield Village, a restored historic community in Dearborn, Michigan. Similar carriage operations add the the appeal of theme parks throughout the country, including the popular horse-drawn trolleys that travel the streets at the Disney parks in Florida and California.

A tram full of people makes a heavy load for this Percheron team at the Kentucky Horse Park in Lexington, Kentucky. The Kentucky Horse Park keeps horses of many breeds on display, holds horse-related activities in their many arenas and buildings, and has a wonderful Museum of the Horse.

An early morning look at a downtown street on Mackinac Island, Michigan. Just an hour later the street was jammed with tourists. The vehicle with the trotting bay horses is a taxi-cab. The vehicle in the background, with the standing roan horses, takes the tourists on a ride around the island.

Mackinac Island is a unique place. Located at the northern tip of lower Michigan, almost underneath the magnificent Mackinac Bridge, it is an island community of 2,200 acres. No automobiles have been permitted on the Island since 1900. The only motor vehicles are a fire truck, police jeep, and some maintenance equipment for the State Park. Some of the 600 permanent residents have snowmobiles which are useful in crossing over to the mainland during the winter when the lake partially freezes.

During the summer months more than 800,000 visitors flock to the Island to shop, bicycle, golf, ride or drive horses, and/or just relax. During these busy months a local tour company operates more than 75 horse-drawn vehicles, using more than 300 horses, to move people and goods around the Island. The food for all these people, and the hay and grain for all these horses, all has to be ferried to the Island from the mainland — and then moved by horse-drawn wagons around the Island — just a mammoth undertaking.

"Business is picking up", as the street-sweepers like to say. It takes a large crew, working full-time, to keep the streets of Mackinac Island free of horse manure — and they do a very good job of it.

Randall McCune Photo

The Grand Hotel omnibus drawn by two Belgian horses makes its way up the long drive to the Hotel.

Bob is one of the more picturesque taxi drivers on the Island. The taxis are all radio-controlled, and they do a good job of moving people around the Island. When the weather is warmer Bob will remove the curtains from the sides of the taxi.

This is the United Parcel Service truck on Mackinac Island. The team waits patiently on the dock as the wagon is being loaded with goods from the incoming ferry. Everything needed on the Island comes in this way, including hundreds of wagonloads of hay for the 300 horses kept there during the summer months.

Jim and Sue Kane give carriage rides in Lake Geneva, Wisconsin, during the summer months. Lake Geneva is a resort community, and people are inclined to take the time for a carriage ride when they are on vacation. Jim bought this horse at the Waverly Sale, and it is pictured being sold on page 30.

Carriage rides usually go on into the evening hours. This entire outfit is well illuminated for safety, with flashing lights behind the carriage and beneath the horse's collar. As a further safety measure Jim Kane is in constant touch with his other carriage, operated by his wife, Sue, by means of a walkie-talkie. Jim is smartly dressed in a black suit, ruffled shirt, tie, and top hat. The carriage is equipped with a bag behind the horse to catch his manure.

Each January, weather permitting, the Blooming Grove Historical Society holds a Winter Horse-drawn Vehicle Rally and Display at the historic Dean House in Madison, Wisconsin. Area teamsters bring their horses and vehicles for two days of fun while, at the same time, they raise money to restore Dean House. The public is invited to come for sleigh-rides on the nearby golf course, and the fees collected for the rides go the the restoration fund. Here Barb Kernan of Deerfield, Wisconsin, pulls a bobsled full of people with her team of Belgian geldings. Large loads like this one earn lots of money for the restoration fund. The handsome bobsled is owned by Dean House, and was built by Ronald Mair of Janesville, Wisconsin.

Janssen Photography Photo

Wayne Dingerson drives the Belgian gelding, Jeb, through Bear Creek with his passengers, Danyah Ashley and Janet Logan. Wayne owns and operates the Bear Creek Horse & Carriage company in Lakewood, Colorado, using eight draft horses and several riding horses to pull a variety of horse-drawn vehicles. Customers can choose a sunset or sunrise hayrack ride, complete with a catered meal and live guitar music, or an exciting coach run up Mt. Carbon Mountain behind four trotting horses, in addition to the normal carriage rides around town.

The Royal Ambassador Shires owned by Tom Schwartz of Mauston, Wisconsin, and driven by his son, Tim. This team recently completed a three year tour of the United States and Canada, performing before 4 million people at 350 separate sites. Along the way they raised $350,000 for various charities. The product that Tom and Tim were promoting was the Shire Horse.

Working with Horses — Marketing Promotions

It's hard to believe that as recently as 50 years ago, during the second World War, there still were horses on the streets of most large cities in the United States, picking up the trash, delivering milk, and performing other chores. So much has changed, and the rate of change is almost more than we can comprehend. Actually, we can't comprehend it; we simply are carried along by it.

There is a part of us that deplores these changes; that cries out for things to remain as they are or were. But there's no stopping change. Life gets ever more complicated. This feeling that life is getting far too complicated must be one of the reasons why people have such a love affair with the Budweiser hitch.

The Budweiser draft horse success story has been imitated many times, and continues to be imitated today. Dick Sparrow has contracted his Belgian hitch out to Coors Brewery, and makes many appearances throughout the country each year on their behalf. Tommy Lawrence has a team of Percherons which visit shopping centers and do parades on behalf of the Southern States Feed Company. The H. J. Heinz Co. has recently revived a proud tradition by assembling a six of black Percherons. And the list goes on and on. New ones start up, and others quit. It takes deep pockets and a serious committment to keep a draft horse hitch on the road.

Caterpillar Tractor Co. used this photo of a pulling horse team taken by the author to capture the reader's attention in a series of ads for their earthmoving equipment.

115

But hitches aren't the only way draft horses are used as a selling or promotional tool. The general public (the vast majority of people who now live in cities or suburbs) is attracted to these big horses. Would Mackinac Island draw such crowds if automobiles used their roads, rather than draft horses? Many businessmen have seen the appeal of the draft horse and decided to use it as selling feature. Pumpkin sellers and Christmas tree farms combine a horse-drawn wagon or sleigh ride with the selling of their products, giving them an edge over their competition.

A pumpkin grower near Milwaukee has Merle Fischer bring 10 or 12 of his Percherons to his pumpkin fields each October weekend, when the weather is nice. Merle hitches 3-abreast to some very large wagons, and a pair to smaller wagons, and hauls the pumpkin seekers out to the pumpkin fields. They pay Merle $1.50 each for the round trip ride, and pay the farmer for the pumpkin. This operation is so successful that they have often had to bring in additional pumpkins, by truck, to replenish the emptying fields. The horses are an essential part of the marketing strategy for the pumpkins.

Bed and breakfast operations use draft horses as part of their promotion, offering sleigh rides, wagon rides, or just plain a chance to pet and brush the big horses. State Parks, National Parks, and tourist areas plan activities which use draft horses to capitalize on their appeal. The list goes on and on. Put quite simply, the public's fascination with draft horses is used as an additional selling feature in many businesses. The only limits are your imagination.

The Historical Society of East Troy, Wisconsin, hired our team to promote their activities in the local 4th of July parade. Justin is driving, and Joe is riding. Mom dressed the boys, dad took the picture and members of the Society rode in the back of the hitch wagon on card table chairs. Similar scenes are played out in literally thousands of parades throughout the country each year, as draft horse hitches are second only to the local high-school band in spectator appeal.

Marge Getchman Photo

Lyle and Marge Getchman operate the Pinehaven Bed and Breakfast on their farm in Baraboo, Wisconsin. There are many attractions in the Baraboo area for their guests, but the Getchmans have not ignored the appeal of their Belgian horses. Their brochure invites guests to "take time to admire the Belgian draft horses kept on the farm…. Time permitting, a wagon ride pulled by the mighty Belgians may be arranged in the summer, or perhaps a sleighride in the winter."

Karen Sanbak Photo

Sixteen guests at the Garland Resort in Lewiston, Michigan, on their way to a Zhivago Night party — a five course gourmet meal 45 minutes back in the woods in the Buckhorn hunting lodge. The grade Belgian mares, Hanna (age 10) and June (age 7) are owned by Karen Sandbak and Keith Fick of Karefree Ranch in Fairview, Michigan, and are being driven here by Keith. The sleigh was built at the Karefree Ranch using a mint condition Stoughton (Wisconsin) running gear purchased at the Waverly (Iowa) Sale.

THE BUDWEISER HITCH

In April, 1933, August Busch, Jr. formed an eight horse hitch of Clydesdales to celebrate the end of Prohibition, and delighted his father by parading the hitch down the St. Louis, Missouri, streets with the first post-Prohibition beer from their Anheuser-Busch Brewery. As the saying goes, "The rest is history". The Budweiser hitch has become an integral part of the Anheuser-Busch trademark and image. Its success as a marketing tool is unquestioned, and is taught in every basic course in advertising.

The Budweiser hitch is now three separate hitches. In addition to the St. Louis hitch housed in a historic 1885 stable they now have a hitch based in Romoland, California, and another in Merrimack, New Hampshire. These three hitches travel a combined 90,000 miles each year, making over 300 separate appearances. The number of people who see them each year, either in person or in the many TV advertisements, is enormous.

Each Budweiser hitch gelding must be 18 hands tall (or taller), three years of age or older, bay in color, with four white stockings, a wide white blaze, and black mane and tail. These animals don't grow on trees. The Brewery maintained a large and vigorous breeding program at their Grant Farm in St. Louis, but still had to scout far and wide, on both sides of the Atlantic, to find replacement geldings for their hitches.

Two recent changes at Anheuser-Busch are worrisome for those who value the support which the Budweiser hitch has given, and continues to give, to the entire draft horse community. In 1990 the breeding operation was reduced from 90 animals to less than 20, and it was moved out of St. Louis to Romoland, California. Soon after, in 1991, August Busch, Jr. died. Mr. Busch was a dedicated horseman, and his influence and support of the hitch was unfailing. There is no doubt that keeping the Budweiser hitch on the road is a very expensive operation. I'm sure it's hard, even impossible, to determine exactly how much beer is sold as a result of the hitch. Let's hope that someone in the Sales Department at the Brewery doesn't decide that they need more commercials with girls on the beach, and that the horses should be cut back to help pay for them. Without Mr. Busch around the question is sure to come up.

The Anheuser-Busch hitch of eight Clyde Geldings.

Draft horses do seem to sell beer. Most of the major breweries in England have Shire horses which are used to promote their beers. Several of these companies still make beer deliveries to pubs near the brewery with antique horse-drawn delivery wagons. For years Doug Palmer took the Carlsburg (Brewery) hitch of Belgian horses on appearances throughout Canada. There are literally dozens of examples where draft horses are used to market beer in North America and Europe.

Rollie Cooper recently retired from the University of Wisconsin, and now spends his summers raising four acres of organically grown vegetables on his mini-farm in Whitewater, Wisconsin. The vegetables are sold at the local Farmer's Market. There is no direct connection between horse farming and organic farming, but the public tends to make the connection anyway. He gets considerable local publicity when he uses his horses in his fields, and this publicity doesn't hurt one bit when it comes to selling his vegetables.

Chip Lawrence driving six grey Percheron geldings owned by his father, Tommy Lawrence (Shore Creek Farm, Roxboro, North Carolina), on behalf of the Southern States feed company. This hitch makes 18 five-day trips each summer and fall, travelling throughout a six state area, doing parades and store appearances on behalf of Southern States.

Southern States Photo

Robert L. Vickrey of Mt. Clemens, Michigan, was a an important member of the draft horse community until his untimely death in 1988. A true gentleman, he held offices in the Percheron Association and the Michigan Great Lakes International, and his Belle River Farm Percherons were consistent winners in the show-ring. This tradition is now being carried on by his son, Robert S. Vickrey. Bob uses his six or eight of Percherons to attract crowds, enticing them to visit their commercial display trailer. After a parade or exhibition the horses are unharnessed and placed in individual stalls set up next to the trailer. People stop to see the horses, and then go inside the trailer to see the commercial display. The top picture shows the horses in their portable stalls, with the ramp on the right leading to the commercial exhibit. The lower picture was taken inside the commercial exhibit trailer. Bob worked for the Michigan Department of Agriculture when these photos were taken, and the commercial exhibit promoted the products grown on Michigan's farms. During the five years he travelled for the Dept. of Agriculture they visited all 83 counties in Michigan, traveling up to 10,000 miles each year, with a total of 24,000 people viewing the commercial exhibit in the trailer.

Photos provided by Robert S. Vickrey

Dick and Joy Sparrow of Zearing, Iowa, take their six of Belgian geldings out to parades, fairs, and other events on behalf of the Coors Brewing Co. In 1991 they made 26 separate appearances, from Topsfield, Massachusetts, to Preston, Idaho — expect to have an equal numer in 1992. The Coors Public Relations Department estimates their hitch is seen by 7,000,000 people in person, and another 6,000,000 on TV and in print. When Dick has the opportunity to do an exhibition drive he shows how the six can back up the wagon to an imaginary loading dock, as was required before trucks replaced horses for delivering the freight. To conclude the exhibition he drives the six around the arena at a full gallop, as he was doing when this picture was taken at Columbia, Tennessee.

Smaller breweries might use smaller hitches of smaller horses. Gene Tylee and his son, Todd, go to about 15 parades and fairs each year on behalf of the Leinenkugel's Brewery of Chippewa Falls, Wisconsin. The horses are half Belgian and half pony, which Gene raises and calls Bel-Ony draft ponies. The wagon is a roll or keg wagon, so named because it is constructed of a series of pipes that allowed the deliveryman to load and unload the beer kegs by rolling them along the pipes. This historic wagon was built about 1890, probably at the Chicago Wagon Works, and is 14' long, 8' high, and 6' wide.

CHARLIE MANNERS TREE FARM

A group of happy customers bring their trees out of the woods at the Manners Tree Farm, New Lyme, Ohio.

Forty years ago Charlie Manners began growing Christmas trees on his farm near New Lyme, Ohio. Ten years later he needed a way to get his customers to the trees, and back again. He decided to use draft horses. Each day, from Thanksgiving to Christmas, up to 14 teams of horses take wagonloads of people out to where the trees are growing. The customers pick out a tree, cut it down, and then drag it to a central location where it is wrapped for easy transport home. Another wagon ride brings them and their newly-cut tree back to their car. Before going home, however, most folks spend some time at the Pine Tree Lodge where refreshments, a roaring fire, and entertainment is available to help everyone catch the holiday spirit. The entire experience is enjoyable, and becomes a tradition that is repeated year after year.

The Manners Tree Farm sells 4,000 Christmas trees annually, and they believe they are the largest such farm using horse-power in the United States.

Kay Demski Photos

An overhead view of the the Manners Tree Farm, with two horse-drawn wagons loaded with customers making their way back to the Christmas tree fields

H. J. Heinz Photo

The H. J. Heinz Company revived an old tradition when they started a hitch of black Percheron geldings in the mid 1980s. Until the late 1920s the Heinz Company kept 150 teams of Percheron horses busy delivering their products in the Pittsburgh area. John Dryer of Avella, Pennsylvania, assembled and manages the eight horse Heinz hitch, traveling throughout the United States and Canada promoting Heinz products. This photo was taken in Calgary, Alberta, during the annual Calgary Stampede. The Heinz hitch wagon is one of the largest hitch wagons in the world, weighing over 6,000 pounds.

Carol Misiaszek Photo

In the mid 1980s Dick Menkins of Tully, New York, traveled 12,000 miles a year in New York State on behalf of the local power company. The program kept 4 people busy on a full-time basis, as it was not unusual for them to hitch six horses 100 times a year, appearing at fairs, parades, cub scout clubs, senior citizen organizations, and other similar groups.

Who can resist a sleigh-ride through the woods with the sun shining
and the new snow heavy on the evergreen branches? Here Jim
Cornish and his son, Jason, of South Harpswell, Maine, take a
sleigh-ride on the Clem Dunning farm. The horse is Molly, a grade
Belgian mare. The sleigh was originally built at the Maine State
Prison, and has been completely rebuilt by Clem.

Elsa Martz Photo

Recreation with Horses — Winter Fun

People who live where the snow falls seem to enjoy hitching up their horses, putting on the sleigh-bells, and going for a sleigh-ride. It's the winter equivalent of the summer parade.

Snow can cause real problems when it becomes too deep or heavy, as we saw earlier in the chapter on winter feeding on western ranches. But in the midwest, east, and throughout Canada when the new snow falls, covering the drabness and ugliness of winter, and the sun comes out making everything sparkle and shine, its time to take a sleigh-ride.

Ardith Hatch Photo

Sandy and Dick, a pair of Belgian geldings owned by Boyd Little and being driven by Clifford Hatch, pull a bobsled full of happy people through the woods near their home in Wentworth Valley, Nova Scotia.

Henry Sarafin driving his two Belgian geldings, Paul and Rowdy, on his Maple Acres Farm near West Chesterfield, Massachusetts. This team weighs 4300 pounds, and Henry uses them for horse pulling, sleigh-rides, hay rides, and a "Hands On" draft horse course which he teaches. Henry has participated in horse pulling contests for the past 40 years, and, at age 72, still uses his team for "environmental logging", working with the Massachusetts Department of Fish & Wildlife.

Louise Oxenhorn Photo

C. J. Aune of Cannon Falls, Minnesota, driving his Percheron / Quarter cross mares, Diamond and Pearl, at the St. Paul (Minnesota) Winter Carnival Sleigh Ralley. C.J. is acting as chauffeur, sitting on a small seat behind the passenger seats occupied by his wife, Geri, and their son, Jerritt. The sleigh is Austrian, and was built around the year 1900.

Claude Roy Photo

Michel Ruel of Saint-Fabien, Montmagny, Quebec, drives his Belgian geldings, King and Sundy, out to the woodlot to haul in some firewood. His two sons, Richard and Martin, get a free ride in their small sled. Michel is a draft horse farrier, and he also works as a lumberjack for five to six months of the year.

Dr. Charles Mayo and his wife, Cari, of Georgetown, Minnesota, driving their Belgian team of Arla & Maggie at the 1992 Beargrease Sleigh Rally held each year in Duluth. This event draws nearly 75 turnouts for two days of fun in the snow each year. Dr. Mayo is a grandson of Dr. Charles H. Mayo, co-founder of the Mayo Clinic in Rochester, Minnesota.

127

Jerome Fry with four of his twenty grandchildren about to take a ride behind King and Prince. The Frys have nine Belgians, and Jerome uses them to rake all his hay and do some plowing on their 200 acre farm. With their son, George, they show their horses at many parades and shows. Jerome and George have built three hitch wagons — and they built the handsome box on the bobsled in this picture.

Kate and Queen, a pair of black mules owned and being driven by Chuck and Judy Carlson of Princeton, Minnesota. This same pair of mules are pictured in their summer coats (without their winter coats) on page 39.

Tom Guderski Photo

Marguerite Pretz with two of her six grandchildren, Kyle and Nicole, bringing home the Christmas tree on their farm near Markesan, Wisconsin. Their sorrel mules, Willie and Waylon, double as pack mules for Marguerite's son, Jim, on his elk hunting trips in Colorado.

Larry Cornelis Photo

George Cornelis of Porthambton, Ontario, bringing home the Christmas tree on a bobsled with his familyl. George is driving his Belgian gelding, Duke, using a European-style (Belgian) harness, and the European method of driving with only one line. The horse is taught to turn right when the line is given a jerk, and to turn left when the line is given a steady pull. The horse is trained to respond this way by first training him with two lines, using these two types of signals — jerking and pulling.

Wayne Rubright with his wife, Elaine, daughter, Kim, and some friends on a sleigh ride near their home in Coeur d'Alene, Idaho. The two grade Belgian mares are 9 yr-old Bonnie (on the off, or right side) and her 5 yr-old daughter, Bell.

Bob Thomas Photo

An old photo from the book Heroes In Harness which illustrates a similar snow roller.

Dave Stalheim of Amery, Wisconsin, with four of his Clydesdale geldings on a snow roller built by Tom Boelz of Clear Lake, Minnesota. Before the days of removing snow from the roads with salt and plows they rolled and packed the snow with large rollers like this.

Dave Schubert of Brainerd, Minnesota, pulling a load of logs with four of his Percheron geldings. Dave and his friends have put on horse-logging demonstrations in both Bemidji and St. Paul, Minnesota. They skid logs, then lift them on the sled with a horse-drawn cable looped over a pully at the top of a log jammer, and move the loaded sled down an iced trail with the team. The runners on the sled are 8' apart, and the sled platform is 12' wide. This load would make quite a stack on a conventional bobsled. The horses walk in an un-iced area between the 8' wide runners. Extra "snatch" teams are hooked on the sled corners to help it start moving (and then cut loose "on the fly"), as the sliding runners generate heat which causes the sled to freeze tight as soon as it stops. Long steel bars are also used to break the sled runners loose when they freeze down.

Tom Mischka drags a Christmas tree home with the help of Jed, a Percheron gelding.

Alex Fraser approaches the ring with his Belgian four at the Draft Horse International Show held each October in Sandpoint, Idaho. Riding with Alex is Roger Rausch. This show is a major draft horse event (over 100 separate classes) which attracts exhibitors from the northwest part of the United States and western Canada. Alex and Kayo Fraser live in Gold Creek, Montana, where they buy, train, and sell hitch horses. Alex designed and made the brass-trimmed, rosewood-colored harness; and they did the finish work on their hitch wagon.

Recreation with Horses — Showing

Draft horse shows are a popular form of recreation and entertainment, both for the participant and the spectator. The number of draft horse shows has increased dramatically in the past decade. Not so long ago the only places you could show draft horses was at the state fairs in the major midwestern states, the Toronto Royal Winter Fair, and a few other regional shows. It wasn't difficult to decide on a show schedule, as there just weren't that many decisions to make. The show season ended in September, unless you were going on to Toronto in November. And since it was a buyers market for the show managements, the horses were taken for granted and premiums were so low as to be almost non-existant.

How things have changed. Literally hundreds of new shows started up, with dozens of county fairs in the agricultural states starting draft horse shows. The Michigan Great Lakes International came along in 1977 and changed the level of premiums offered. It became a seller's market, with the horse owner being the seller. Show managements could no longer take the horses for granted, as there now was a choice of where to show, so conditions improved. Finally, with so many new shows, there is no longer a show season — it lasts all year long.

Showing draft horses is something I know a little about, as our family has done quite a bit of it. Also, I have taken a lots of photos at draft horse shows the past 10 years. With a little luck I hope to follow this book with one on just showing, and include some information that should be useful to those who are just getting started in showing. We'll see. So this chapter will be relatively short.

The leaders in Dr. Joseph Hunt's show hitch of sorrel mules wait patiently for the call to enter the ring at the Michigan Great Lakes International Show in Detroit. Dr. Hunt practices general medicine in Carleton, Michigan, but his avocation is the promotion and enjoyment of mules

Henry Junkans drives the Argonaut Farm Shire hitch at the 1991 Britt, Iowa, show. On the box with Henry is Randy Riemer. The Argonaut Farm, owned by Virginia Stainton, is located near Glenwood Springs, Colorado. This is one of the top hitches in North America today, with wins at all the major shows. When the judge doesn't pick them, the crowd usually does. Henry, his wife, Sheila, Randy, and Ms. Stainton are all to be congratulated on assembling and showing this outstanding hitch. This is an amazing achievement when you remember how relatively few black Shires there are. Just a few years ago this would have been considered impossible.

Vern Cook (driving) and Glen Schrader bring the Miller Container hitch in the ring at the Boone County Fair in Belvidere, Illinois. This show, held in early August, is one of the largest county fair draft horse shows in the midwest

Mike and Meg Kelly of Johnson Creek, Wisconsin, leaving the ring area in front of the grandstand at the Walworth County Fair, Elkhorn, Wisconsin. Their horse is a Belgian stallion named Justin. The Elkhorn Fair brought back the draft horses in 1983, after an absence of over 50 years. Their return was a big success, with crowds of 500 people per hour filing through the barns during the peak weekend days. Literally hundreds of county fairs throughout the country have added draft horse exhibits to their programs during the past decade.

Draft horses (and Mules) are also shown at Carriage shows, where turnouts are judged on their appearance, conditioning, ability to negotiate a timed obstacle course, and willingness to meet certain hazards (water, bridges, caged animals, etc.). Here Neil Kibler of Neenah, Wisconsin drives his team of Belgian geldings over a small bridge obstacle at the American Heritage Driving Event. Neil placed first in the Training Level-Pairs Division, beating three other Morgan and Lipizzan teams.

Ross Beattie and his granddaughter, Emily, on their way to winning the Belgian mare team class with Monalisa and Miss Myra at the Michigan Great Lakes International (Detroit) Show. The Beattie Brothers of Stayner, Ontario, have dominated the Belgian mare hitch classes at this show for years. The "Detroit show" is the biggest and best draft horse show in North America, with 1,000 horses (and mules) and 200 exhibitors. The future of this show is now in doubt, however, as the state funding which had supported the show has been withdrawn.

Steve Gregg drives the Harry Farr Belgian four-abreast hitch to a win at the Live Oak Invitational Draft Horse Show held in Ocala, Florida, each February. The Farr family is from Dunnville, Ontario. The Live Oak Show is relatively new, having started in 1988. It, like the Britt, Iowa, show, is for hitches only — no halter classes.

Linda McMain Grange is driving a McKeehan Farm entry to a win in Belgian Ladies Cart at the Toronto Royal Winter Fair. The Toronto show, held each year in November, is an elegant affair, with ladies in fur coats and men in tuxedos sitting in reserved seats to enjoy the jumping horses, coaching classes, and draft horses. There's lots of pomp and ceremony — and it's fun. A win at Toronto was "as good as it got" until the Detroit Show started up in 1977. Linda and Craig Grange now live in Delmar, Iowa, where they raise, buy, train, and sell outstanding Belgian hitch horses — and raise 350 acres of corn and soybeans.

This is the last time I will bore you with a picture of my kids — I promise. This is Karla (grey) and Brunhilda being driven by our youngest son, Joe — the first time he ever drove in a show. Beside Joe is his older brother, Justin. We showed our home-bred mares in cart, team, unicorn, and four at most of the major shows in the Midwest. I broke and trained the horses at home, and our boys got the fun of driving them at the shows. The wagon is homemade, using an antique running gear and rebuilt wheels.

Dave Adams of Britt, Iowa, winning the Supreme Champion Six Horse Hitch competition at the Boone County Fair in Belvidere, Illinois. With Dave is Ed Carlson. Dave had an outstanding Percheron hitch in the early 1980s, and his six was undefeated in 1981 and 1982 at all the major shows throughout the U.S. and Canada.

Marion Young leaves the ring at the National Clyde Show held during the Wisconsin State Fair after winning the Ladies Cart Class driving Joker, a gelding owned by the David Carson Farms of Listowell, Ontario.

The late Harold Clark ushered in the modern era of draft horse showing by setting the standards of excellence at Meadowbrook Farm that are still being strived for today. Many of today's winning horses go back to horses he bred, and many of today's winning showmen started their carreers with him. This photo of Harold was taken in the 1940s, and was provided courtesy of Jim Richendollar.

Audrey Bunston of Schomberg, Ontario, clearly enjoys driving her Belgian gelding, Doug, in the Ladies Cart Class — and Doug obviously enjoys it too. Together they are difficult to beat, and usually end up at the top of the class.

Bud and Mike, two Belgian geldings owned and driven by Ray Garb of Beaver Dam, Wisconsin, pulling at the Jefferson, Wisconsin County Fair. These large horses are 9 and 14 years old in this photo, with a combined weight of 4,750 pounds. Each March, as the pulling season approaches, Ray works his horses for 3 to 4 hours each day. By June they are in pulling shape, and the workout is cut back to an hour daily. Horsepulling is not just a weekend activity. Ray has been horsepulling for the past 35 years, and his teams do very well on the midwest circuit.

Recreation with Horses —
Horsepulls

Horsepulling evokes strong emotions in some people. It is an activity that people often feel very strongly about, either for or against. But like it or not, it surely is a popular and legitimate recreation activity with draft horses.

In the midwest the horses are required to pull the weight a distance of 27 ½ feet while staying between two boundry ropes or marks. The distances are different in other parts of the country. The teams which succeed in pulling the weight the required distance are asked to do it again, this time with more weight. The winning team is the one that pulls the heaviest weight the longest distance. The weight may consist of a sled or stone boat, loaded down with cement blocks or other ballast, or it may be a dynamometer truck — a special truck that is pulled backwards while a series of weights and pulleys exerts a measured load on the pulling team.

In the past there has been some drug abuse with pulling horses, just as with human athletes. Most of this has been eliminated now, and the horses are tested for drugs on a random basis at many of the larger pulls to make sure they are drug-free.

Generally speaking, a horse will quit pulling once he senses that the load is too heavy for him. This is true of any horse, and any load. The owner of a pulling team wants his horses to be confident that they can do it — otherwise they won't be able to do it. Because of this the horses are seldom asked to do more than they are able, whether it be at the horsepull or at home, during their training. It is this mistaken belief that pulling horses are pushed beyond their abilities that makes some people dislike this activity.

A team of mules pulling at the Annual Mule Days Celebration held each April in Columbia, Tennessee. This celebration attracts hundreds of mules and over 200,000 spectators for 4 days of springtime fun.

Donna Thomas of Waitsburg, Washington, with a pulling team of Shire geldings owned by her father, Mel Anderson, at the Draft Horse International Show at Sandpoint, Idaho. Donna is an all-around teamster who has been driving horses since she was 12 years old. Walking alongside her, giving moral support, is her brother, Bill Anderson.

Photographer Unknown

Terry Sherman Photo

Left: In Wells, Vermont, the horsepull is called a Log Scoot. The load is measured in board feet and each team has three chances to move the load 12 feet. Here we see Hollis Tucker from Wakefield, Rhode Island, crossing with the winning load.

Todd Sowle of Beloit, Wisconsin, pulling his team at the Jefferson County Fair. This is a typical setting for horsepulls — a dirt track in front of a grandstand, amusement rides in the background, a waiting pick-up truck with more weight, and the other teamsters and their families watching the action from card table chairs alongside the track.

142

Sharon Fenton Photo

Ward O'Boyle of St. Louis, Michigan with his Belgian team called Rock & Jerry, at the Champion, Michigan, horsepull. This is a good view of the Dynamometer truck. The numbers indicate that Ward is pulling the equivalent of 3,550 pounds.

Doug Ward of Marshall, Wisconsin, making friends with a pulling horse owned by Ray Garb called Mack.

The grandstand at the Walworth County Fair in Elkhorn, Wisconsin, holds 4,000 people, and it's always full for the horsepull each Labor Day morning. Here Ken Markham of Elkhorn moves his team up to the stoneboat loaded with cement sacks as the crowd watches. Kenny is the son of Henry Markham, also a horsepuller. This sport seems to get in the blood, and sons frequently start by helping their dad, and then go on to have their own team.

The Great Milwaukee Circus Parade is a real extravaganza, with 50 antique, restored circus wagons pulled by over 200 draft horses and a few camels, mules, and donkeys; 800 riding horses; a half-dozen elephants; and assorted caged tigers, snakes, hippos, bears, etc. Here we see Jim Rupple driving the late Rolland Ruby's Belgian six pulling the France Bandwagon, built in 1919. Sitting alongside Jim is Jake Ruby, Rolland's son.

Recreation with Horses — Wagon Trains and Parades

I've never gone on a wagon train, but from what I've heard they sound like a lot of fun. The preparation part must be a little like going off to a five day horse show, but without the competition. You have to think about what to take — what's absolutely necessary, both for you and the horses — and then try to figure out how to squeeze it all in. It's an exercise in priorities, in getting things down to the bare essentials. Then, when you are off, you enjoy a complete change of pace from your regular schedule. No telephones, mail, or routine chores. Every day becomes an adventure, with new things to see and new people to meet, and a completely new routine. There is time to think and to talk, and time to do just nothing. It sounds great. I think I'll try it.

Parades are a little different. The preparation and planning is not quite as critical when you will be back home again that night. Parades can be lots of fun, especially with an enthusiastic crowd. After our first Milwaukee Circus Parade I was on an emotional high for a week. Some parades are big deals, like the Rose Bowl Parade or the Milwaukee Circus Parade, and some are small, informal affairs, like the local July 4th parade.

Parades are potentially dangerous situations, with crowds of people who don't understand horses and unfamiliar sounds and sights that can make the horses spook. Taking the horses to town and driving them there before parade day is a good idea, if it can be arranged. If you are driving more than one horse it would be well that several had taken part in parades before. And you should always have someone walking alongside, or an outrider, to help in case there is an emergency.

Rick Maage with his team of 8-yr-old Belgian mare mules, Kate & Nel, taking part in a wagon train in the Custer National Forest near Ashland, Montana.

145

Golda Condron teaches the fourth grade in the Ochoco Elementary Schoool in Prineville, Oregon. Her students got an unforgettable history lesson when they took a two-day wagon trip covering 16 miles, with the students walking most of the way. Two students at a time got to ride a few minutes each day in the covered wagon owned and driven by Raymond Guthrie, also of Prineville. They traveled cross country part of the time, and followed an old stage coach route for the rest. The students dressed in old costumes, and ate the same type of food the pioneers ate from the same tin plates and cups used then. A jug of cream was tied on the side of the wagon, and the rough ride turned it into butter.

Golda Condron Photo

Jan Fraser Photo

Kai Christianson of Polson, Montana, rests his team of Belgian geldings at the top of the mile-long Grundy Hill on the annual Westmont Wagonner's Wagon Trail Trip.

Susan Velin Photo

Tom and Margery Ingraham of Glendive, Montana, with their team of Belgian geldings, Pat and Mike, on the trail during the Great Montana Centennial Cattle Drive. The 1989 Montana Cattle Drive took place to commemorate the 100th anniversary of the admission of Montana into the United States. About 2,700 cattle were trailed the 60 miles from Roundup to Billings, over a 6 day period, with 208 wagons, 3500 draft horses and mules, and 2500 people taking part in the event. The running gear for Tom's wagon was purchased new in 1915 by his great-uncle and is pretty much in its original state. The box dates from the 1930s — the bows and cover are new. The Ingrahams also use their team to feed cattle in winter and cultivate potatoes in summer.

Jennifer Tonn Sternhagen Photo

Martin and Willa Tonn of Carlos, Minnesota, about to do some parading with Rowdy, their part Morgan and mostly Percheron gelding. The buggy is a light Depot wagon — the two seats are easily removed for another trip back to the depot to pick up luggage or freight. The harness is an antique light draft harness, sometimes called an Express harness. The log barn was built by Martin's Great Grandfather in 1874, and housed 8 milk cows, 4 horses, and 30 big loads of loose hay. Authentic outfits like this are great crowd pleasers in parades.

147

The 40 horse hitch was revived in 1972 by Dick Sparrow of Zearing, Iowa, for the Great Circus Parade — the first time anyone hitched 40 horses since the Ringling Brothers Circus did it in 1904. It is now driven by his son, Paul. The wagon which Paul is guiding through the streets of Milwaukee is the Two Hemispheres Bandwagon, the largest circus wagon still in existence, built in 1902. The "forty" is re-assembled each summer for the Circus Parade, with many of the horses and their current owners coming back to Zearing to do it all over again. In the oval picture, pretty well hidden by their helmets, we see Paul with the lines, Dennis Megger beside him, and behind them, as brakeman, is Charles P. (Chappie) Fox, father of the Great Circus Parade.

Eugene Eisenschenk Photo

Richard Notsch of St. Joseph, Minnesota driving his Belgian geldings, Dick and Don, in the local July 4th Parade. Sitting alongside Richard is his brother, Jerry, with Jerry's son, Randy standing behind. The Weber farm wagon was beautifully restored by Richard. This scene is so typical of the informal parades that take place in small towns throughout the U.S. and Canada.

Merle Fischer of Jefferson, Wisconsin, drove his eleven Percherons in tandem (in single file) in the 1991 Milwaukee Circus Parade. They are pulling the Bostock-Wombwell Menagerie Bandwagon, built in the 1850s — the oldest wagon in the parade. The key to this hitch is the lead horse, Rex, a sensible horse who listens to Merle's instructions, and with the stamina and strength to keep the 10 horses behind him strung out in a tight, straight line. Rex is seven yrs old, and has been in the Circus Parade since he was two.

Lois Winter Photo

Scott and Astrid Gottschalk of Minneota, Minnesota, driving their 16.2 hand sorrel mules across the Yellow Medicine River near the Minnesota-South Dakota border. Scott was the wagon master of the annual Camp Courage Wagon Train which raises about $100,000 to benefit crippled children each year. Scott and Astrid spend about 20 days each year on wagon trains, dressing in authentic buckskin and pioneer clothing.

Fred "Bud" Sauter fulfilled a life-long dream when, upon retirement, he bought a small farm near Tryon, North Carolina, fixed it up, and got his first pair of draft horses. He shares this "dream come true' with others by giving rides to groups and individuals, with the help of his neighbors, Pat and Ray Malone. Here Ray is driving Bud's team, Matilda and Clementine, on a pleasure drive, with Bud sitting in the back and Pat standing on the step. The vehicle is a cut-under 9 seat vis-a-vis with a fringed top and roll-down curtains. It is hard to find a more worthwhile activity for a team than giving rides at a children's camp, retirement home, or other similar place.

Chuck Hearon Photo

Jim and Ruth Lotan in the lead wagon of the Bitterroot Centennial Wagon Train, part of the 1989 Wyoming centennial celebration. The Bitterroot train travelled over 400 miles, and took six weeks to complete. In the process they crossed the Continental Divide at 7,000 feet elevation. Some doubted they could make it, but all wagons made it in excellent shape. Jim retired from the U.S. Forest Service in 1987 so he would have more time to work with his horses. When someone asks him what he uses his horses for, he replies "any excuse I can think up."

Gary Wells Photo

A large Mule Days Celebration is held each Memorial Day weekend at Bishop, California. Here is the entry of the Lane Ranch & Co. of Lancaster, California in the Bishop Mules Days Parade. This parade is touted as being the world's largest non-motorized parade, with 200 units and 800 mules participating.

You can see a wide variety of activities at a field day or plowing match. Here Max Preuss of Ixonia, Wisconsin, hooked his Belgian team, Butch and Pat, to an antique water wagon and took a load of water out to the steam engine which was providing the power for a threshing machine.

Recreation with Horses — Field & Work Days

Edward Heinze of Dazey, North Dakota, demonstrates his horse-powered well drilling rig. This is the type of new and different activity that people putting on field days are always seeking to show and demonstrate.

Farmers love to get together to catch up on the gossip and trade stories. Normally they work by themselves, with their family, with little contact with their neighbors. This way of life made the occasional times when they would get together to share work, such as during threshing or baling time, so very important to them.

There isn't a whole lot of work-sharing on farms now. Taking its place, at least in part, are the hundreds of antique machinery shows, threshing reunions, draft horse field days, and plowing matches held throughout the country, especially during the autumn months. Some of these events are strictly for tractors, some are just for horses, and many have both. Some are elaborate affairs just like a County Fair, but without the midway rides and games of chance. Others are quite simple — just a group of neighbors getting together at someone's farm to do some field work and visiting.

A draft horse field day is show-time for the farmer. Overalls and work harness are appropriate.

153

Evelyn Hanson Photo

Carl Madsen of Webb, Iowa, plowing with six Belgian geldings at the Threshermen's Show in Albert City, Iowa. Carl's horses are well protected with fly nets and with burlap coverings on their necks to help keep them cool. Behind Carl's hitch another team picks up oat bundles for the threshing demonstration.

Bill Spaulding of Frederick, Wisconsin, drives three 14-hand molly mules to a disc at a field day sponsored by the Wisconsin Draft Horse and Mule Association, one of two they hold each year in the northwest corner of the state. Bill's jacket proclaims his partiality to mules.

Ernest Schulz, Marc Gravert, and Brian Daldorf operate a horse powered baler at the Great River Thresher Days Festival held each year on the third weekend in July in Miles, Iowa. Ernie's Belgian gelding, Jake, is stepping over the plunger which packs the straw or hay in the bale chamber. As the horse makes his circle the plunger retracts, and the operator forks more material into the chamber. The bales are tied by hand with wire.

Some draft horse field days attract large crowds, especially those which have been going on for many years. The Minnesota Plowing Match is one of the largest, and it is very well attended. At some field days it's almost impossible to get a picture without crowds of people in the background.

This photo was greeted with strong feelings, both for and against, when we used it in our 1983 calendar. We've avoided using a foaling picture ever since. It is always surprising how differently people will react to the same photograph. At the time I thought it was the most sensitive and beautiful foaling picture I had ever seen. I still think so. Those who are offended can tear out this page, as they tore out the calendar page 10 years ago.......The brand new floppy-eared foal with its hind legs still in the birth canal is already beginning to dry off. The mare, now that the crisis over, is now looking back, concerned with her new baby. It's morning, and the waiting is over — a new life is starting. The mare is Bonnie, a Clyde/Belgian cross. Her foal was named Roantree Henry Snickers. The event took place at the home of Amos and Jude Holdsworth of Hyde Park, New York, the owners of Bonnie.

Jude Holdsworth Photo

Foaling, Foals and Kids

The birth of a new foal, like any birth, is a glorious event. The wonder of it all continues to amaze me, even after watching and worrying over so many. The mare's relief when the foal's hips emerge, the foal's first futile attempts to stand, the mare's patience as the foal looks for the nipple, and the mare's fierce protectiveness during the first week or so — all this and so much more are scenes that can't really be described; they must be seen and experienced. Those who have the opportunity to observe this miracle are indeed privileged, and never take it for granted.

Although the process is beautiful the foal itself, like most babies, is only beautiful to its mother. Birth is a messy business, and the new born foal takes on this messiness. But after a couple of days it begins to put some flesh on its bones, learns to use its ridiculously long legs, and is fun to watch. From then on it changes each day, growing so fast that it seems the halter has to be let out every week or so.

Children seem to have a natural attraction to foals, as they do to other animal babies. Horses seem to have a natural concern about children, and will often tolerate behavior from a child that they would not accept from an adult. The horse seems to sense the innocence and helplessness of a child, and it often acts accordingly.

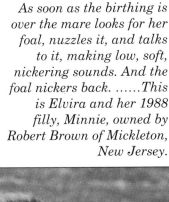

As soon as the birthing is over the mare looks for her foal, nuzzles it, and talks to it, making low, soft, nickering sounds. And the foal nickers back. ......This is Elvira and her 1988 filly, Minnie, owned by Robert Brown of Mickleton, New Jersey.

Maxine Brown Photo

157

Photos for these two pages are from, starting at the upper left and going around clockwise, Thelma Farr, Lela Roby, Todd Bingham, Lola Kruse, Meredith Hodges, Lela Roby, and Betty Priske.

Appendix

Note: This appendix has been printed on a separate sheet so it will be easier for us to make changes, as they become necessary, during the life of this printing of the book.

Breed Associations

Belgian Draft Horse Corp. of America
P.O. Box 335, Wabash, IN 46992
(219) 563-3205
Vicki Knott, Secretary

Percheron Horse Assoc. of America
Box 141, Fredericktown, OH 43019
(614) 694-3602
Alex T. Christian, Secretary

Clydesdale Breeders of the U.S.
17346 Kelley Rd, Pecatonica, IL 61063
(815) 247-8780
Betty J. Groves, Secretary

American Shire Horse Association
Box 669, Glenwood Springs, CO 81602
(970) 945-9145
Sheila Junkans, Secretary

American Suffolk Horse Assoc.
4240 Goehring Rd, Ledbetter, TX 78946
(409) 249-5795
Mary Margaret Read, Secretary

Canadian Belgian Horse Assoc.
Rt 3, 17150 Conc 10, Schomberg, Ont.
LOG 1T0 CANADA, (905) 939-1186
Barb Meyers, Secretary

The American Donkey & Mule Society
PO Box 1210
Lewisville TX 75067
(972) 219-0781

Canadian Donkey & Mule Assoc.
RR 2 , Site 1, Box 15, Rocky Mountain House, Alta. T0M 1T0 CANADA
Karen Anderson, Secretary

Magazines & Periodicals

The Draft Horse Journal
Box 670. Waverly, IA 50677
(319) 352-4046
Lynn Telleen, Editor
A quarterly magazine which is essential for anyone interested in draft horses.

The Small Farmer's Journal
P. O. Box 1627 , Sisters, Oregon 97759
(541) 549-2064
Lynn R. Miller, Editor & Publisher
A quarterly magazine featuring articles on horse farming.

Heavy Horse World
Park Cottage, West Dean, Chichester, West Sussex P018 ORX, England
Diana Zeuner, Editor
A quarterly magazine covering draft horses in England.

Driving Digest
PO Box 110
New London, OH 44851-0110
(419) 929-3800
A bi-monthly magazine covering all types of driving horses, ponies, and mules. Significant draft horse and mule coverage in each issue.

Percheron News
A quarterly magazine for Percheron Assoc. members.

Belgian Review
An annual magazine for Belgian Assoc. members.

Clydesdale News
An annual magazine for Clydesdale Assoc. members.

Feather and Fetlock
Box 9, Cremona, Alberta, TOM ORO, CANADA, (403) 337-2342
Bruce A. Roy, Editor & Publisher
A quarterly magazine covering the draft horse scene in Canada.

Western Horseman
Box 7980, Colorado Springs, CO 80933
Many articles on both draft horses and mules, particularly in a western setting.

Rural Heritage
281 Dean Ridge Ln., Gainesboro, TN 38562
(931) 268-0655
Gail Damerow, Editor
A quarterly magazine including much draft horse material.

The Brayer
A quarterly magazine sent to American Donkey & Mule Society members.

Mules & More
P O Box 460, Bland, MO 65014
(573) 646-3934
A monthly magazine devoted to mules.

The Saddle Mule News
P O Box 1573, Boyd, TX 76023
(940) 433-2729
A magazine published 5 times a year for saddle mule enthusiasts.

Directory

The Reach
P O Box 932, Kendallville, IN 46755
(219) 347-8223
An annual directory for Horses-in-Harness

Books, Calendars, Videos

Mischka Farm
PO Box 224, Oregon, WI 53575
www.mischka.com
1-877-MISCHKA or (608) 835-6853
Bob & Joseph Mischka
Publisher and distributor of draft horse & mule books, calendars, and videos.
Free color catalog available.

Supplies, Machinery, & Equipment

Meader Supply Corporation
23 Meaderboro Rd, Rochester, NH 03867
1(800)-446-7737
A complete line of products for the draft horse owner. Free catalog available.

Taborton Draft Supply
54 Taborton Rd, Averill Park, NY 12018
(518) 794-8287
A complete supply of products for the draft horse owner. Catalog available.

Gifts and Novelties

Permanent Impressions
2182 Bruce Rd, Utica, OH 43080
Cathy & Greg Grandstaff
Apparel with Draft Horse & Mule designs. Other gifts.

Organizations & Newsletters

Carriage Operators of America
517 Hallet Rd, East Stroudsburg, PA 18301
Eileen Pasquin, President
Devoted to helping carriage operators. Annual convention.

North American Horse and Mule Loggers Assn.
8307 Salmon River Hwy, Otis, OR 97368   (541) 994-9765
Devoted to helping horse loggers. Annual convention.

Horselogger's Newsletter
c/o Gregg Caudell
Box 34-C, Keller, WA 99140
(509) 634-4388
A newsletter with tips for horse loggers.

Index of People

Index of People (Continued)

Index of People (Continued)

Index of Photographers

Index of Photographers (Continued)

The remaining photographs were taken by the author.